Also by Kathleen Rusnak

Caring for the Caregiver:
A Spiritual Approach for the Professional

————◄◊►————

Kathleen Rusnak's lectures
are available on CD

Because You've Never Died Before:
The World of the Dying

Loss, Grief, and Elder Care

Before They Forget:
Maximizing the Spiritual Possibilities of Alzheimer's

————◄◊►————

www.thebrickwall2.com

Evelyn,

Walk in Love,

Kathleen Rusnak

BECAUSE
you've
NEVER DIED
before

BECAUSE
you've
NEVER DIED
before

≈

SPIRITUAL ISSUES
at the END
of LIFE

Kathleen J. Rusnak, Ph.D.

Because You've Never Died Before:
Spiritual Issues at the End of Life

by Kathleen J. Rusnak, Ph.D.

Published by
The Brick Wall 2, Inc.
21 Mohawk Trail, PBN 263
Greenfield, Massachusetts 01301
www.thebrickwall2.com
(603) 359-8078

For information on bulk purchase of this book,
contact the publisher at thebrickwall2@yahoo.com

Some material included in this book is adapted
from previous works by the author.

ISBN: 978-0-9846001-4-4

Design and composition: www.dmargulis.com
Cover image: Johanne Fradette, yojojo47@hotmail.com

Second printing 2011

MANUFACTURED IN CHINA

In memory of Anne Bernhaut (1947–2006),
my dear friend and second-generation Holocaust survivor,
whose tears, laughter, love of life, and concern for others
live on in these pages

In memory of my mother, Joyce Rusnak (1929–2011),
and father, Irwin Rusnak (1924–2011),
neither of whom thought they helped in any way
with the writing of this book. But they did.

CONTENTS

FOREWORD

YOU MAY HAVE opened this book looking for help and guidance. Perhaps you are dealing with having received a sudden, life-changing, terminal cancer diagnosis. Perhaps you have just been advised by a thoughtful, caring physician that your elderly mother's condition is unresponsive to treatment, her prognosis for survival is short, and hospice care is needed.

Reading about death is not a recreational pursuit. It is unlikely that you would pick up *Because You've Never Died Before* at the neighborhood

Barnes & Noble unless you had the need to know about a terminal diagnosis, whether you are the patient or the family member, friend, or caregiver of such a patient.

Death and dying are not topics that easily attract readers. The author of a book about facing a terminal diagnosis must have experience in dealing with spiritual matters that affect dying patients; a scholarly background in philosophy, psychology, and theology; and an eminently readable writing style that sustains the reader's interest. Kathleen Rusnak has those qualifications, and her ability to entertain while she educates is truly a gift.

Because You've Never Died Before is written in a conversational, storytelling style and with compassion and well-placed humor, very much as a pastor might speak with her congregation. After describing the spiritual changes that begin with the receipt of a terminal diagnosis, Kathleen provides for her readers compassionate insights and constructive suggestions that are equally useful to a dying patient, a friend or family member trying to help with a specific problem, and a professional caregiver.

By depicting the abrupt disruption in what had been a routine and ordinary life, Kathleen dramatically and effectively shows us the differences between the life of an individual before receiving the diagnosis of terminal illness and his or her life after being told that death from a specific medical condition is certain or near. Few of us are equipped to deal with crises or situations in which death is the only—and perhaps imminent—outcome. Learning more about our deeply embedded fear of and anxiety about death, our specialness, and our "not just yet" attitude about our own death can help us make better decisions as we travel through the jungle of conflicting emotions that result from loss and grief.

Regardless of the specific scenario, Kathleen helps us understand that almost all patients and families eventually accept the reality of approaching death and that their need for spiritual and emotional support increases as that time grows near. This is particularly true for those who are suffering painful anticipatory grief and are consumed with the impact that such a crisis is having on them as they cope with a cascade of emotions. Knowing what a person with a terminal illness is feeling and thinking may enable family members to concentrate more on exploring and understanding that patient's spiritual needs, which in turn can lessen the burden of their own pain as they help their loved one.

For those of us in the healing and caring professions, *Because You've Never Died Before* has the potential to become a classic resource; it offers spiritual, philosophical, and theological wisdom that is useful to everyone involved in helping people who have a terminal illness. This book is not a dull, dry tome. A master storyteller, Kathleen presents much that is familiar to us about death and near-death awareness, and as she does so, she takes us to a deeper understanding of the spiritual issues affecting dying patients, and she shows us how to better address those issues.

Because You've Never Died Before is valuable to anyone facing death, as all of us eventually must: for the patient who is fighting to stay alive; for the patient who is ready to accept death quietly, as a timely and appropriate end; and for friends, family members, and healthcare professionals struggling to understand the needs of a dying person. In truth, this is a book for us all.

—*Jack McNulty*, MD, FACP, FAAHPM

New Orleans

www.palliativecare-la.org

PREFACE

I DO NOT REMEMBER who the psychiatrist was—even a face—only that it was a man. I do not remember the interview, only that the evaluation was sent to my supervisor regarding my suitability for clinical work and my placement recommendation. The summary read, "Kathleen is afraid of death. I recommend she do her CPE in a hospital setting." I was furious at such an analysis and simply could not fathom where he got this idea. I tore up the evaluation in anger and asked again for a prison setting.

My placement was in a hospital in Chicago.

All seminarians are interviewed by a psychiatrist before being admitted to the required summer clinical pastoral education (CPE) training. Three clinical choices were available at that time—to work with clients in a hospital, psychiatric, or prison setting. Hospice settings were still years away in the mid-1970s.

I had requested a prison setting, explaining that I wanted to deal with clients on the intellectual level where I thought change was possible. Physical and mental illness did not interest me. I was even considering the possibility of becoming a CPE supervisor as a career option of ministry, to work with seminarians. I was deep into theology, psychology, and philosophy. I loved intellectual play and insight. I loved carrying books around.

When I first entered ministry with the dying, in New Jersey in the mid-1980s, I thought it was a ministry like any other ministry. I was deceiving myself. After my CPE experience, there was something in me that wanted to face death, think about it, and understand it. I thought about death often, not in some morbid way, but as the great event that made life so important; how we lived it, what choices we made. Death gave life purpose and meaning. The fact that we die, I realized, was one of the reasons I entered theology and ministry in the first place. Death, I believed, was why religion existed. Religion was about ultimate issues: it could explain why we were born, how we should live, how we should treat each other, what our purpose and meaning in life were all about, and who our maker was. Early on, I simply wanted to think about death, not get too close to it, as in being around sick or dying people. I did not realize until the death and dying movement came to America that only by being around and working with persons who were facing death could one experience the great event of impending death. Working with dying patients compelled me to look at these ultimate issues.

I want to offer you a framework that has emerged over the years I have worked in different hospices, giving spiritual care to patients who were dying. If you work with the dying, you may already know much of this. Putting it into a framework helps to define, name, put into order, and give meaning to the spiritual experiences of our patients. I do not claim to have discovered something new. I have named and framed our experience of the spiritual dimensions expressed by those who are dying. This book confirms what you know, gives order and meaning to what you have experienced, and equips you to better understand, feel more comfortable with, and create positive interventions for your patients. If you have not worked with the dying, this book will lead you into the depths of life as it is experienced by people who learn they have a terminal prognosis. This is an opportunity for you to gain from the wisdom and insight of the dying for your own life now.

Author's Note

Stories are based on composites of real patients, whose actual identities have been disguised. Any similarities to situations you have experienced personally are coincidental, as these archetypal scenarios recur in many families. Quoted conversations are based on my recollections of many encounters with real patients over the years and are not from transcripts.

ACKNOWLEDGMENTS

My DEEP THANKS go to all of those who have attended my many lectures on this subject and encouraged me to put these thoughts into print. Their desire for a book made me realize the value it might have for all those caring for and working with the dying.

My heartfelt thanks to Claire F. Pace, hospice nurse-practitioner, who stood by me throughout the many years it has taken to write this book, reading and correcting early drafts of chapters, talking ideas through, encouraging me at times when I wanted to give up, but never giving up on me. Her steadfastness has been a gracious gift to me.

I am deeply honored that my colleague and dear friend Rabbi Eugene Korn graciously read and advised on each section of this book pertaining to Judaism and Jewish thought. However, any errors in these sections are of course my own.

My special thanks to Valerie Lake, hospice nurse, colleague, and dear friend, for her encouragement to keep writing, her careful reading of the final draft, and her useful observations; and to my new colleague and friend, the Rev. Dr. Shane Phelan, an Episcopal priest whose remarks were valuable to the completion of the manuscript.

Without my editor, Dick Margulis, this book would still be only a draft in a dream. What you are holding is the result of his expertise and skill, from editing the text and challenging my thoughts and arguments for clarity, to the beautifully set type, cover design, printing quality, and binding. Dick's know-how, efficiency, and care are his gift to would-be writers like myself. Katharine Wiencke, a skilled editor in her own right, corrected the proofs with a meticulous eye, and Rossinna Ippolito indexed the book.

While I have been a student and admirer of Bonhoeffer and Frankl since early adulthood, I would like to recognize the following authors for providing me with the factual knowledge of their lives that I needed to illustrate the progressive and cumulative losses they endured to complete chapter 5, "Who am I?"

Anna Redsand (*Viktor Frankl: A Life Worth Living*), Ferdinand Schlingensiepen (*Dietrich Bonhoeffer 1906–1945: Martyr, Thinker, Man of Resistance*), Stephen Haynes (*Bonhoeffer for Armchair Theologians*).

To all of these, I say thank you.

BECAUSE

you've

NEVER DIED

before

CHAPTER I

Two Worlds

There are two worlds. You and I live in the world of the living. Our patients live in a very different world. They live in the world of the dying. It is a world that we do not know from the inside, because we've never died before. It is a world that we cannot fully inhabit—not as nurses, social workers, chaplains, volunteers. We cannot inhabit this world or empathize with its residents because it is a world different from ours.

We do not know what it is to die.

Having never gone through the dying process, the living cannot fully get into the mindset,
or see through the eyes, of those who are dying.
This mindset can only be fully realized after a
radical existential shift takes place. This shift cannot take place in the imagination. It must really
happen for the effects of the event to be transfor-
mative.

Look at our common experience of the terrorist attacks of September 11, 2001. If you had
been asked on September 10 to imagine what your
feelings or experiences would be if two passenger
airplanes were to fly into the World Trade Center
towers, causing them to collapse, your imagination could not even have come close to identifying
the emotional impact of the actual event unfold-

ing before your eyes. The next day, witnessing this terrorist attack in person or on TV caused a shift to take place in many of us, and we knew that life could never be seen or experienced through the eyes of September 10 again.

You have to differentiate the world of the dying from the world of the living. Are you aware of what makes your world a living world? We are not always aware of our world. Often we just live routinely and unthinkingly. It isn't easy to discover what makes our world a living world. The way we think and act is something we take for granted, as just the way life is. We are no different from the dying in this. The dying are also not conscious of what frames their world. A terminal prognosis throws a person into an unfamiliar world, a world that must unfold in all of its newness on a daily basis. The impact of September 11 unfolded for each of us daily. We could not have predicted how terrorism would affect our personal or national worlds. We did not know what to expect ahead of time.

It is the same for those who are dying. They know their world has changed, but they cannot anticipate what those changes will be, because they have never died before either. There are worlds that all of us know—for example, the world of grief. We have all experienced loss at various times in our lives. We have lost a favorite thing, a job, a loved one. We all know grief. But we have never died and have never been dying. It is a world we don't know, but it is a world that we are journeying toward. Those who have had a near-death experience (NDE) or have miraculously recovered from a terminal prognosis may have the best understanding. The world of the dying is a world of *nearing death awareness* (NDA). Described by two hospice nurses, Maggie Callanan and Patricia Kelley, in their now classic 1992 book *Final Gifts: Understanding the Special Awareness, Needs, and Communications of the Dying,* NDA takes place as one experiences the process of dying. NDA includes such phenomena as reviewing one's life in its entirety, asking what contributions one has made in life, and being visited by deceased relatives. NDA differs from NDE, in which a person is declared to be clinically dead, is revived, and returns to life to tell us about what it was like to have died (for example, out-of-body experience, being in the presence of lights, moving through a tunnel, and breaching the boundaries of time and space). This book is about NDA, as terminal patients do not die and return to tell us of their experiences but rather tell us of their experiences as they approach death.

Despite our fear of death, there is something that attracts us to the world of the dying: we are interested in ourselves and in what will happen to us and to our loved ones. We ask questions such as: What will I go through? What issues will I deal with? How will I feel? Unless we die suddenly, the world of the dying will be our world. When we look at the world of the dying, it isn't a *them* world; it is an *us* world. We are repelled by the thought of dying because of our fears; thus we want to *know,* because one day this is the threshold we too will cross. Our secondary interest is our wanting to know how to care for the other—the parent, spouse, or friend who will one day be dying.

Frameworks are important. Think of the framework of *psyche* that Freud discovered. By giving names to the different components of the psyche, he was able to give shape to chaos. He named the psyche's parts and defined how they were connected to, and independent from, each other. He gave us the words *conscious, unconscious, id, ego,* and *superego.* These components give us the big picture and the particulars that allow us to understand what is happening inside our minds.

Freud did not *invent* the psyche. He wonderfully *discovered* its various components and the way these components work.

If I were to ask you to give me a framework that constitutes *living*, a framework that differs from a framework that constitutes *dying*—what would you answer? When I ask my colleagues and students this question, they at first state the obvious components of being alive: breathing, thinking, hoping, and feeling various emotions. When I counter that the dying also breathe, think, hope, and feel, they are stumped. The dying person lives inside a different framework, a different worldview than those who have not received a terminal prognosis. The dying person sees and lives life in a way they could not have imagined *before*. We, the living, live in that *before* world. It is living on the other side of *before* that makes the dying person different from the living person.

Yes, the dying are living too, living *until* they die. Those who decide to work with dying people are often not conscious that their work is experienced as work with the *other*, who is not us. When I told this to a nursing class, a student said, "But we are all terminal, aren't we?" His question was an attempt to see us all on a smooth continuum from birth to death. This view denies the impact that receiving a terminal prognosis has on a person's world, a prognosis that changes everything. To say that we are all terminal is not the same thing as to *know* that we will die in four months! If we have not entered into that final chapter of life, life *after* we have received a terminal prognosis, we are not in the world of the dying.

I want you to imagine that this morning, before starting to read this chapter, you received a phone call from your doctor. She insisted that she needs to see you today to review the results of your recent tests. You have known and respected your doctor for many years, trusting in her care and expertise. You have not been well. You recently underwent a series of diagnostic tests, including a biopsy. These tests were designed to determine the cause of the symptoms you've been experiencing—difficulty swallowing, severe nausea, shortness of breath, and increasing pain. The doctor's call raised your anxiety and you went in immediately to see her. As kindly as possible, she revealed that the tests indicate that you have cancer—advanced cancer! With intense compassion and concern, she told you that palliative care is the only option and that you need to get your affairs in order, because it appears that you may have less than six months to live.

This is difficult if not impossible to imagine because we really cannot put our whole self into that situation. We cannot feel fully the shattering impact of such news. This is the world the dying enter.

CHAPTER 2

THE BRICK WALL

I WANT TO DELINEATE for you the boundary between the world of the living and the world of the dying. Through the discovery of the world of the dying, we discover the world of the living. Our primary goal is to discover the spiritual issues that emerge, so that the dying can die well and the living can live better.

How do I understand this world? My patients have been my teachers.

THE IMPORTANCE OF METAPHORS

Metaphors are powerful. They express in symbolic language the depth of raw feeling and emotions that cannot be directly expressed in words. I want to begin with a metaphor often used by patients who find out they have a terminal prognosis. The first time I heard a patient say, "When the doctor told me I had less than six months left to live, it felt like I hit a brick wall," I didn't hear it. The second time a patient said that to me, I heard it for the first time. And then I read this metaphor in a hospice nurse-practitioner's master's thesis on suffering. The interviewed patient said, "I can be having a good time and it comes slam, like a brick wall, that, well, you're going to die."[1]

I'd like us to look at this metaphor. *It is this metaphor that separates us from our patients in the world of the dying.*

This particular metaphor is not one you will find in the death and dying literature. So it's not a metaphor that one dying person has read somewhere and is using. It comes from within—it comes from the experience. New experiences create a new language. New experiences create metaphors. And even though the metaphor is created, that doesn't mean we who use the metaphor or have the experience know exactly what we mean by it.

For example, the first time you lost a significant person through breakup or death, you may have expressed your pain through the common metaphor "my heart is broken." It's a metaphor we use without knowing all the ramifications of what it means to *live* a broken heart. At the beginning I don't know what it is to live a broken heart tomorrow, what it will look like a month or a year from now, or how it will transform me in the future. But I use the metaphor because it expresses the depths of a pain that cannot be expressed otherwise.

So when the dying say, "It felt like I hit a brick wall," they are expressing in a metaphor a reality they have never experienced before and have no other words for. Why? Because they have no other language for what they have never experienced *before* they were dying. On the other hand, those of us who work with the dying have seen patterns emerge. What I offer you is what patients have taught me: what they have experienced, what I've observed over and over and over, and what makes their experience *spiritual*.

GETTING BENEATH THE METAPHOR

I want to get beneath the metaphor "the brick wall," because the experience of hitting a brick wall is what separates *us* in the world of the living from *them* in the world of the dying. Yes, this is a politically incorrect construct, us and them. But in this world, the world of the dying, there really is a separation between us and them.

DENIAL: NOT YET

I toy with the audience when I present this material. I ask people to raise their hands if they believe that one day they will die. Everyone laughs as they raise their hands (if only to not look foolish). I preface my next question by requesting that people not be philosophical in answering, because of course we all know that we could die today by being struck by a car while crossing the street, and because we all know that we don't *know* the future. Then I ask, "How many of you believe that you have at least five more years to live?" Regardless of age, nearly everyone raises their hands. In my experience, ninety-year-olds raise their hands. We know we will someday die—but not yet!

Someone inevitably asks, "But aren't we all dying the moment we are born?" I try to guess what motivates the asking of this question. Is it a way to dismiss the us versus them by claiming dying as part of the continuity that takes us from birth to death? I counter that we learn in psychology many developmental theories, all espousing that from the moment we are born we are developing, not dying. The simple movement of time forward does not mean we are dying. All of life meets death, but from the moment we are born we are struggling to master developmental tasks. We are becoming, not dying. Death can come at any age, suddenly or forewarned. So, we are still left with our question. If our patients know they will one day die, why do they hit a brick wall? Why don't they just say, "Oh yes, I have been dying all along anyway," or "This is what I have been waiting for"?

I did a presentation on this topic for hospice volunteers. The day after my presentation the volunteers wanted to set up an information table about hospice care in the center of their mall, and they asked if I would accompany them. Well, you can imagine! The small kiosks in the center of the mall were filled with the usual products—cell phones, scarves, eyeglasses, stuffed animals, and the like. Hospice information seemed quite incompatible with this environment. It certainly was not the most likely place to give out this information. People started coming over to our table and asking what we were selling. A predictable pattern of response emerged. The first volunteer would say, "We are about palliative care." The visitor would respond, "What's that?"

The next volunteer would say, "Hospice." Again, the response was "What's that?" Finally, another volunteer would say (in exasperation), "This is about death and dying." Each person, unfailingly, upon hearing this trilogy of responses, would hold up their hands as if pushing something away and, while simultaneously chuckling and backing away from the table, repeat the words "Not yet!"

When I was a younger pastor, before my involvement with hospice, Hans, a seemingly healthy man in my congregation, telephoned in a panic and asked that I come to his house. When I arrived, Hans was visibly angry. His anger quickly mixed with tears as he spoke. He told me that he had just been diagnosed with a terminal illness. "Why me?" he roared, as if a great injustice had crashed in on him. At the time, I was 36. Hans was 93. I found myself carrying on an internal conversation while standing there listening to Hans. I saw myself shaking him by the shoulders, as if to wake him to his senses, and I heard myself say, *Why me? You are ninety-three years old, for goodness' sake! What do you expect—to live forever?* Luckily, I didn't utter a word; I managed a poker face. What I realize now is that if I had asked Hans that question, he would have responded, "No—but not yet!" When someone asks the question, "Why me?" it is not a question we are expected to have an answer to. Rather, it is a crying out from within: *I thought I had at least five more years. Why now? Not yet!*

DENIAL: NOT ME

I toy with my audience again, this time telling them I have another question but know they will refuse to raise their hands to answer it, out of embarrassment. I ask, "How many of you think that you are more special than the person sitting next to you?" Roaring laughter and movement again acknowledge the commonality of our individual egos' claim to superiority.

Deep down, I suppose I believe that I'm a little more special than you. I have no problem imagining another person's death. In fact, I hear about people dying every day, and I have no problem imagining their deaths. But I can't imagine my own death.

When we are young, we believe we are immortal. For example, when eighteen-year-olds go to war, many don't believe they will die. During the Gulf War, I saw a young marine interviewed on television after her husband, who was also a marine and who had been missing in Iraq for nearly a week, was found. When she was asked her feelings about the situation, I remember her saying, "All of us here at the fort know that some of us will die, some of us will be wounded, and some of us will be POWs, but not one of us here ever believes it will happen to me." They go boldly into battle believing, in the beginning at least, that an exciting adventure awaits them and that somehow death is meant for others but not for them. I once heard a mentally and physically healthy seventeen-year-old boy start chuckling because he knew how silly his words were about to sound. He said, "I'm the first person living who will never die." While we may think he was just joking, and while he also believed that death would be an eventuality, I knew when he said it that he *believed* it emotionally, even though intellectually he knew it was not true. I remember believing the very same thing about myself when I was young. Even now, when we are middle-aged or elderly, and we *know* death as a hard-core reality, we cannot imagine death for ourselves.

We cannot imagine not existing, not being. Death is far off.

———◄○►———

I recently asked my father, who was in the first wave at Normandy (Navy, LST), what it was like to be an eighteen-year-old going to war. Now eighty-five, he remembered that he thought the war was going to be an "adventure." With his chin quivering, holding back tears, he added, "I thought I was invincible." On D-day he knew differently. As they approached the beach, my father said, they saw soldiers falling left and right in battle and masses of bodies on the beach and floating in the water. He said he started to pray the Twenty-third Psalm as the battle raged on in front of his eyes and as their ship drew closer. As he was praying, he remembers thinking to himself, "I wonder what my wife and children *would have looked* like." While he did not die, as he expected to, for the first time ever he believed he could.

LOSING SPECIALNESS

I want to tell you when I lost that feeling of specialness. Throughout my whole life, I had 20/15 vision. Not 20/20 vision. But 20/15. I had super eyes. I could see things other people couldn't. Of course, I thought I was very special. Then I remember waking up one morning as an adult to find the words in the newspaper very blurry. This was no trivial matter for me. Because I worked in hospice, every symptom I experienced, from sore throats to difficulty breathing, I imagined was cancer. With blurred vision, I just knew I had a brain tumor. After all, I had 20/15 vision! Nothing was wrong with my eyes. The head nurse at hospice, knowing of my hypochondria (associated with many of us who work in hospice) told me I needed to see an eye doctor. I did, still believing that I had no ordinary problem. At the conclusion of the eye examination the doctor looked at me and in all seriousness said—my heart was just beating wildly, and I thought, *Okay, how long do I have?*—"You need glasses." And I remember how taken aback I was by that. I mean, I didn't understand it. I just looked at her, and after a lengthy pause said, "Why?" She asked me, "How old are you?" And I said, "I'm 43." And she said, "That's why." I'll never forget that day or the inner indignation that I felt. Inside I was saying, *What do you mean, that's why? You mean everyone in their forties needs glasses? You mean I'm like everybody else? Me, Kathleen Special Rusnak!*

It was a turning point for me. I was forced to acknowledge my commonality with other human beings. The message was clear. You are not special. You are like everyone else. You can get hit by a car. You will die. You can get cancer. You are deteriorating. You are not different from everybody else.

We all need that experience somewhere along the way, that experience that makes us realize, *I am not invincible. It can happen to me. I will not live forever.* Death is that great boundary experience, as the philosophers, psychotherapists, and theologians tell us, that causes us anxiety because it threatens our uniqueness and "specialness."

There is a wonderful 500-year-old midrash (rabbinic teaching) about the death of Moses, retold by Mordicai Gerstein in his illustrated 1994 children's book, *The Shadow of a Flying Bird: A Legend of the Kurdistani Jews.* In this embellished story based on the biblical text, God tells Moses, who is 120 years old, that it is time for him to come home. Moses, shocked by the news, begins to argue with God. He lists the reasons that he should be allowed to continue living. He has not been to the Promised Land yet; he hasn't seen the yet unborn children and grandchildren God has promised his lineage. He just has more to do, see, and experience. When God rejects his reasoning, Moses begins to bargain with God, begging for more time. When all else fails to change God's mind, God commands angels to bring Moses home. Because of the greatness of Moses, each angel refuses to be responsible for ending Moses' life on earth. Weeping, God finally has to be the one who comes and takes Moses home. One hundred twenty years old!

EXISTENTIAL SHIFT

What happens when you get a prognosis that you are dying? Let me transpose what patients have told me and what I have observed into a first-person narrative.

If I were told today that I have three months to live, let me calculate ... it means that because this is February 2010, I will die in the middle of May 2010. It means Christmas 2009 was my last Christmas and Thanksgiving was my last Thanksgiving, although I didn't know it at the time. It means that this will be my last Easter and my last winter. I won't see summer again. It means what I planned to do and the places I was going to speak at next fall will all be canceled. The vacation I planned? Gone! Everything I planned, gone! It means I have three months left to live! Me. I am going to die at 58!

This is what flashes through a person's mind when they get the news. They hear, see, envision, *Twelve weeks left. Twelve more Mondays, Tuesdays, etc.*

Right in the middle of living my life, this brick wall stands right in front like an insurmountable obstacle. Nonnegotiable! The end! I can't go over it. I can't go under it. I can't knock it down. I won't wake up from this bad dream. Finished!

Hitting a brick wall causes a shift to take place in reality. A brick wall event separates life *before* from life *after*. Martin Heidegger, a twentieth-century German philosopher, talked about this shift. He said that events like death—knowing that we are going to die—cause a shift within us from the "forgetfulness of being" to the "mindfulness of being." We in the world of the living all too often live in the forgetfulness of being. We don't think about our deaths, not very often anyway. Oh, we do if someone we love dies, or when we first start hospice work, at least for the first six months, or every now and then, but we soon become task-oriented with all the regulations and the overload of work. Our patients know this about us, too. They know it because they used to be us. They know that at 5:00 PM, while they are lying in their beds, we are living our lives, making dinner, hugging our kids, watching TV, laughing, doing homework, and planning our lives.

The majority of us do not awaken in the morning, sit at a desk or at the kitchen table, take a piece of paper and at the top of the page write the question, "Who am I?" No, the first thing we do, after our morning routine, is make a list of what we have to do today and add on to the lists for this week, this month, and this year. In the midst of all the to-dos and the reading of this book, your mind may wander to all the other things you have to do besides the immediate—what the weather will be like next week, plans you have, friends to meet, calls to make, and so on and so on. In other words, the forgetfulness of being is the routine that we live.

When a person learns they are dying, when they hit a brick wall, a shift takes place. They move from the forgetfulness of being to the mindfulness of being. This is a spiritual shift. It is spiritual because the questions and thoughts of the person are now existential in nature. *Who am I? What was my purpose? Did I have a purpose? Did I waste my life? Did I love? Was I greedy? Did people love me? Will I be remembered? Did I make a difference?* (These are the kinds of questions the great religions of the world try to get us to think about for ten or fifteen minutes a week.) This is the mindset of our patients, of people who are dying, whether or not they express this to us in words or are able to articulate it clearly to themselves. The metaphor says it all. *I was living my life. I was going about my business. I found out I was dying. Everything changed. I started thinking deeply about the meaning of life and the meaning of my life. I departed from the world of the living. I am in a different place now.*

Let us look at the spiritual shift that occurred September 11, 2001. One poem circulating on the Internet in the first week after 9/11 noted that on September 10, we forgot to kiss our kids goodbye as they left for school, didn't say I love you to our spouses as we left for work, wondered how the stock market would do. On September 12, we kissed and hugged our kids, said I love you to our spouses, wondered about life's purpose, asked about spiritual things. The shift separates life *before* from life *after.* It is accompanied by the words "Nothing will ever be the same again." We live in a post–9/11 world. We have a post–9/11 mentality, a post–9/11 spirituality. We no longer live in a pre–9/11 world, one that is marked by a feeling of being invulnerable, innocent, and carefree. Books about September 11 are titled simply, *After* and *Since September 11.*

———◦———

A less known example that separates *before* from *after,* but one with enormous ramifications for both

Jews and Christians, is that of the Holocaust and the founding of the State of Israel. I have taught post-Holocaust theology to college students and given lectures on the subject to both Jewish and Christian clergy and laypeople. I have been surprised at how few, especially among Christians, are aware of the Christian teaching of contempt.

"Teaching of contempt," a phrase coined by the French Jewish historian Jules Isaac, refers to the negative theological attitude and false teachings of Christianity about Jews and Judaism, teachings that allowed and even sanctioned horrific behavior toward Jews from the time of early Christianity up to the Holocaust. The persecution and suffering Isaac's family and the Jewish people endured in Christian Europe during the Second

World War—the brick wall event known as the Holocaust—precipitated, for Isaac, a long look back over the centuries of the teachings of Christianity regarding Jews and Judaism. He wanted to know how the Holocaust could happen in Christian Europe.

As a Jew, Isaac was not interested in Judaism or Jewish culture. He regarded himself as a Frenchman through and through, even though he never denied that he was Jewish. When he lost his position as inspector general of school instruction in France in 1940 because he was a Jew, he was shocked. His worldview and interests changed. His look back over the history of Christianity took him first to reading the Gospels in the New Testament and then to studying early Christianity;

he then published a short article on the subject. During this time he and his wife moved into hiding. His wife was arrested by the Gestapo during his absence from home one morning. She managed to get a note to Isaac from the transit station in Dracy (on her way to Auschwitz, where she died in 1945), which said simply, "Complete your work, which the world is waiting for." Devastated, he spent the next decades dedicated to this endeavor, in memory of her, his daughter, and other Jews who died in the Holocaust.

What he discovered in his research informed and influenced the changes in Christian theology that would take place *after* the Holocaust. In his 1948 publication, *Jesus and Israel*, he claimed that what the Gospels taught and what Christianity taught regarding the Jews, Judaism, and Jesus' Jewishness were different from each other. Nowhere in the Gospels could he find that Jesus denounced his Jewishness, Judaism, or the Jewish people. Nowhere could he find that the Jewish people should be cursed to wander the earth homeless because they rejected Jesus as the Messiah. Nowhere could he find that the Jewish people in every generation were to be cursed for having Jesus crucified (the charge of deicide, the act of killing God). Isaac claimed these were false teachings, not biblical teachings.

In 1960, Isaac had a brief and positive meeting with Pope John XXIII. He spoke to the Pope about the development of the teaching of contempt within Christian teaching, and he praised the Pope for his efforts already effected to rectify the church's teachings on Judaism. The turning point from *before* to *after* came in the Second Vatican Council five years later, in 1965, in the document known as *Nostra Aetate* ("in our time"), which rejects the deicide charge against the Jewish people, and which rejects the assertion that the covenant between God and Israel was replaced (called replacement theology, substitution theology, or supersessionism) by a new covenant in Jesus Christ. Indeed it now contends the covenant between God and Israel is a living covenant, not abrogated. *Nostra Aetate* inspired most Protestant denominations to reappraise their own theology toward Judaism and the Jewish people, a negative theology which had been seen as the norm and as positive *before* the Holocaust, in a new light *after* the Holocaust.

For Judaism, the Holocaust prompted a looking back over Jewish thought on the subject of theodicy, the justification or defense of God's goodness and justice in the face of evil. Because all theodicies defend God, evil was attributed to the free will given to humans by God. Ultimately, the question of theodicy in the face of evil is the question "How could God let this happen?" or "Where is God?"

Jewish thinkers differ in their views as to whether the event of the Holocaust radically shifts Jewish thinking on God's nature. Why did the God who rescued his people from slavery in Egypt not rescue them in the Holocaust? Those who hold on to Judaism *before* the Holocaust do not blame

God for what happened in Christian Europe. They blame the Christians, or the Nazis. Eliezer Berkovits, in *Faith After the Holocaust*, does not blame God for failing to intervene, but says to Christians, "All we want is for you and your people to keep their hands off of us and our children." Berkovits claims that many Jews either returned to faith, acquired faith in God, or died witnessing their faith in God, in the camps. Berkovits does not view the Holocaust as unique but as another catastrophe, albeit larger than the others, along the continuum of Jewish catastrophes suffered. This implies that Judaism, as is, can already adequately respond theologically to the Holocaust and isn't nullified or modified by it.

Other Jewish thinkers do view the Holocaust as unique, unprecedented in the number murdered, in the calculated and malevolent planning to exterminate *all* Jews; and in that the deed was accompanied by a cultured European people. For them, the event cannot be addressed by Judaism *before* the Holocaust. Richard Rubenstein, in *After Auschwitz,* claimed that the traditional belief in an omnipotent God was no longer possible. "God is dead," he said. Rabbi Neil Gillman interprets this to mean, for Rubenstein, that "the way we have conceived of God and his relation to humanity and particularly to Israel no longer works." Rubenstein says, "After Auschwitz, what else can a Jew say about God?"

Still others, such as Emil Fackenheim, claim that the Holocaust has added something new, one more commandment to the 613 that the Jewish people are already commanded to keep. This last one, number 614, is to not give Hitler a posthumous victory by leaving Judaism, but to survive as Jews and to help the State of Israel survive.

Rabbi Irving Greenberg, another major theological voice after the Holocaust, claimed that the Holocaust and the State of Israel are modern revelations for both Jews and Christians, demanding that they reconsider the original biblical covenant and begin to view each other as partners to promote life rather than death, which the Holocaust represented.

Finally, Elie Wiesel, well-known Holocaust survivor and writer, has espoused the paradox of belief that exists for many Jews following the Holocaust. Here are a few of his claims that I've collected:

"Where was God in all this? It seemed as impossible to conceive of Auschwitz with God as to conceive of Auschwitz without God."

"The God who gave us the covenant at Sinai took it away in Auschwitz."

"How could God be in Auschwitz? How could God not be in Auschwitz?" (I heard him say this at a commencement ceremony at Upsala College in East Orange, New Jersey, in the 1990s, before the college closed in 1995.)

"I still believe in God, in spite of his bad behavior."

The above is only a smattering of Christian and Jewish ideas after the Holocaust but a prime example of how a brick wall event can cause a shift from before to after, a shift that awakens the soul of the individual, or the collective, to a more authentic life. While my own personal and scholarly interests have taken me to the subject of the theological implications of the Holocaust for both Jews and Christians, it was only through my work with the dying and the discovery of the brick wall experience that I understood why such changes occurred.

FROM THE PERSPECTIVE OF DEATH

The realizations that *I'm not special, not yet*, and *I still have five more years to live,* together with the existential shift that separates *before* from *after*, are all indications that most of us in the West avoid thinking about, facing, and preparing for our own deaths.

This taboo of death naturally discourages many of us from allowing death to enter into our conscious daily living. How many of us say to ourselves, as we begin a new day, "I know death will come. It could come today. I will live this day with deep awareness and deep joy, with loving kindness and with helpfulness to my fellow human being. I cannot really ever own anything, and those that I love, I will one day be separated from. Let me live life from this perspective today"? Instead, I have heard people say, "Oh, don't be so morbid. What good is it to think about death? How depressing! Go enjoy yourself." Yet thinking about death need not be morbid. It is not a place to dwell. The simple daily awareness that I will die and that everything, even the people I love, I cannot ever really possess would indeed change the way we live. This kind of thinking is not only a step in the direction of preparing for death but also in living life more realistically—without jealousy, without greed, without competition, and with awareness that we each have the same desire for a good life. No one is more special than another.

In 1974, the Connecticut Hospice became the first hospice in America.[2] Since then, hospice care has become an accepted medical model, with payment for palliative care made by Medicare since 1982. The word *hospice,* for many, has become synonymous with death. It still rings of the taboo subject of death to many Americans who do not want to hear that word. "When I heard they wanted to put me on hospice," said one woman, "all I heard was a death sentence." "Don't mention the word hospice," said the spouse of one of my patients. "He doesn't know he is dying." The latter is a common request of family members to hospice staff. To deal with this dilemma, in order to give patients the care they need, many hospices have pre-hospice services. These services give patients the same interdisciplinary care and pain management as hospice care but allow some continued treatments. In other words, they allow the denial to continue, even when it is clear that cure or even longer life will not result from treatment. In fact, some treatments, such as certain kinds of chemotherapy or feeding tubes in some instances, hasten death. Yet, it does mean that the word *hospice* is never used or that death is not discussed. People die on pre-hospice programs, which are often given euphemistic names, such as Support Care, Bridge Program, or Hope Program. One in three dying persons enrolls in hospice in the US, but the statistic is deceptive if one assumes from it that death is becoming more accepted in society.[3] Families and patients, more often than not, enter hospice programs reluctantly. Many families opt for hospice care on the last day of their loved ones' lives, sometimes within the last hour, indicating how difficult it is to come to terms with dying. This late acceptance of hospice care also greatly limits the help the family or patient can receive from the hospice team regarding the dying process and all the tasks that can be accomplished for both family and patient before death. The most valuable help at this point is what the family can receive in the thirteen-month bereavement care that follows.

I do see hope, however, in our culture. Hospice does offer an alternative model of care that is slowly ingratiating itself into our death-denying culture. Its great companion in this endeavor is Buddhism. While Buddhism has some history in our country before the 1960s, it became quite popular during this era, when many traditional values were questioned. Because Buddhism is a religion that sees life from the perspective of death, and whose premises derive from that end, Buddhists have become the "experts" on death in our society. While there are several Buddhist hospices in America, the Buddhist influence in the hospice movement is huge.

In 1997, I attended a conference, The Art of Dying II: Spiritual, Scientific and Practical Approaches to Living and Dying. It was organized by the Tibet House and the New York Open Center. That was the conference where I first learned of Buddhism's deep involvement in the death and dying movement in America and the reasons for it.

Buddhism focuses on the alleviation of suffering, compassion, letting go (detachment), living now through the practice of mindfulness, and preparing for death so that one can live well and die well. Buddhists also believe that all human beings are equal and that we all want the same thing—happiness and the alleviation of suffering. This means that no one is perceived as special—an idea that hits those of us who die in the West very hard. Buddhism looks at the person in a holistic way, as mind, body, spirit.

Hospice and Buddhist philosophy are taking root in our society, as attested to by 4,200 hospices and an ever-growing number of Buddhists—both Asian and American adherents and converts. This may lead to a shift in the Western mindset and attitude toward death that in turn changes the way we die. Hospice philosophy, like Buddhist philosophy, adds holistic *comfort care* to a single-vision scientific–biological–medical model, where cure continues to predominate, where the body is center focus, and where still too many people die alone in hospitals and in pain. Holistic care means that body, mind, and spirit are of equal importance in the care of someone dying; pain management is central; and people die with dignity. Holistic care means an interdisciplinary team is needed that can address the physical, psychosocial, and spiritual dimensions of the person. The unit of care consists of family members alongside the patient. Death is not seen as the enemy to avoid or defeat. It is not seen as failure, but as a natural part of life. Hospice neither hastens nor delays death, but manages pain, on all levels, to give comfort care.

I also believe that the hospice movement and the growing number of Buddhists in the West have begun to bring out the deeper and more spiritual aspects of Western religious traditions. Many American Buddhists are Jewish or Christian. At conferences where I give presentations, attendees often approach me to comment on the rich inner meaning I give to Christian and Jewish stories and to tell me that they have left their faith traditions. Some tell me they are now Buddhists. When I probe deeper, most do not belong to a Buddhist community but adhere to its philosophy, have read a book, or do mediation. Yet Christianity and Judaism have their own history of mysticism and spirituality that is not acknowledged in the mainline church or synagogue.

Many Jews and Christians drawn to Buddhism's philosophy, spirituality, and meditative practices have been able to go back to their religious traditions and discover the deeper spiritual realities that exist within them but are not emphasized or taught. One Jewish Buddhist said to me, "I really didn't understand Judaism until I became a Buddhist. Judaism seemed so abstract and self-centered; I'm thinking of the 613 commandments I had to keep to be a good Jew. Buddhism focuses on helping others, not keeping commandments and worshipping God. But what I found out was how similar Judaism and Buddhism are. Both are about living ethically, repairing the world—

what Jews call *tikkun olam*—and helping others, and both teach 'love your neighbor as yourself.' Buddhism helped me to understand many different parts of Judaism." A Christian Buddhist attendee said to me, "I left the church years ago, tired of feeling guilt every time I didn't go to church or didn't live by the rules the church said I had to. I didn't experience any spirituality. Buddhism was attractive because it talked about God being within us and said that every moment is a holy moment, that everything is sacred, and that I should be aware of every moment. Then I learned that these ideas are not foreign to the Christian faith. Jesus taught that our bodies are the temple of God and that the kingdom of God is within us. I learned about the contemplatives in Christianity's history and those that exist today. Buddhism helped me understand what being a Christian is all about."

These views and those of other adherents to a Jewish–Buddhist or Christian–Buddhist way could bring a renewal to the Western religious traditions that so many perceive as "dry bones," or as just plain irrelevant. Compassion, respect, living in the present and not worrying about tomorrow, meditation, and dying with dignity are not only the vocabulary of Buddhism. They are the vocabulary of Judaism and Christianity, too.

For example, in my experience as a hospice chaplain, most patients I encounter, those with and without a religious faith, have little or no understanding of death and dying; and they therefore come to their dying in denial, refusing to discuss their impending deaths with their families (avoidance). They are unprepared to deal with the wave of spiritual issues that naturally arise.

Many refuse the chaplain's visit because they think they will be judged; or they feel religion has let them down by, for example, denying them Holy Communion because they remarried following a divorce; or they feel that religion and spirituality are irrelevant in their lives. Buddhist ideas can bring out the best of the spiritual dimensions of Judaism and Christianity, thereby giving hospice patients hope for a positive and deep spiritual experience, one that is compassionate and nonjudgmental.

"Hitting the brick wall" indicates the mindset that prevails in our society—our denial of death (our conviction that we always have five more years, our belief that we are special, our feeling of invincibility)—and thus determines the spiritual issues that emerge from that mindset. While we may look at Buddhists as the experts in facing death, the current Dalai Lama says that Buddhists who don't really practice, even though they have been in monasteries and have been learning all the right things all their lives, are also not prepared for death and will have a hard time letting go. It isn't what religious label we give ourselves that matters, but whether or not we adhere to the deeper spiritual, contemplative, and compassionate values that our religions teach. Our challenge is to find how we can live a deeper, more authentic spirituality, the way many die in hospice programs throughout the United States.

CHAPTER 3

No Future and No More

WHEN YOU HIT a brick wall at the full speed of life, you are not only stopped abruptly, but you fall back shattered and in shock. Lying on the road of life, you stare up at a huge brick wall, panoramic in scope. *You cannot see around it, over it, or beyond it.*

NO FUTURE

You realize that whatever lies beyond the brick wall, the *future*, is blocked from sight and experience forever. The once anticipated future is *no more.* It is blocked, and the new smaller future is in some other direction not yet visible to your mind's eye. For the moment you are stunned and shattered. You have left the world of *before,* the world where you could look ahead.

THE WORLD OF THE LIVING

It is natural for us to look to the future. We hope that by our actions we can find happiness, whether that happiness be a romantic relationship, the company of friends, or our dream career, home, car, and other acquisitions. Most often we see that happiness as something to work toward, something that is in the future. The world of the living looks forward to a never-ending slew of new experiences, acquisitions, and encounters that will bring happiness and fulfillment.

You can see whether you are part of this *living in the future* worldview by answering yes to the following questions: Do you have any plans made beyond the next four months? Are you looking to improve your career? Do you have a vacation planned for the next year—or for the next two years? Is your current work a steppingstone for your next goal? When you wake up on a Monday morning, are you thinking about Friday and weekend plans?

Many of us think happiness is always around the next corner, somewhere in the future. The result is that many of us find it difficult to find happiness and contentment in our present circumstances.

How far ahead do most of us plan without being conscious we are doing so? In Western culture in general, we are people who are tempted daily to live in the future. We live for tomorrow, for the academic degree we will get, for the career we will pursue, for the car we will buy, for the vacation we will take, for the home we will buy, for the children we will give birth to, and for our retirement years. In our culture, it is hard for many of us to live fully in the present, appreciating the preciousness and richness of the moment's encounter. It is easy to wish away whole blocks of time to get to this future of ours. We wish away daily business meetings, the travel time it takes to get somewhere, whole workdays, whole weeks, and even whole years. How often do we hear people planning for holidays or other big events, while saying "I can't wait until it is over"? We plan, we think in the future, and we often dwell there.

A friend's son was entering his freshman year of college. When I asked him what he was looking forward to in this new beginning, he answered, "To graduating. I can't wait to get a job and have my own apartment." When I asked, "What about the four years it takes to get there? What about them?" he answered with short certainty, "Just get through them."

As a pastor, I usually ask the teens in my confirmation class what they want to do in life. I am surprised when some answer, "Retire," and "Make money." When I share this with other pastors, they say they receive similar answers to this question. When I pursue these answers with the question, "But what do you want to do in life in order to get to your retirement?" the answer is also short and unthoughtful: "Just make a lot of money." "But how?" I pursue. "Win the lottery" comes the response, or "There's lots of ways to make money." Perhaps it is telling that one of the most common regrets that patients express at the end of life is that they worked all their lives to live their dreams in retirement. Those of us who work with the dying have often heard the sentiment

"We worked and saved all our lives so that when we retired, we could travel, spend time with each other and our kids, and finally do what we always wanted to do. Now, it's too late."

It is from the dying that those of us who work with them learn to live more fully in the moment, not to wait to do significant things after a retirement that may never come, and not to expect there to always be time *later*. The abrupt shock of not having a future signals the lack of preparation we have for dying, in our culture.

We occasionally see this bit of wisdom— often posted in surprising places such as the wall of someone's office: "The journey is the destination." While Eastern influence is a growing trend in our society, and in my view, a positive influence, for most of us, the journey still remains only a means to the destination—"Are we there yet?"—even if we would like to give the journey the same status.

We find it hard, if not impossible, to imagine the deep turn, lasting and unexpected, that takes place in the dying person's psyche when the future, the place of all of our endless hopes and dreams, disappears, never to be retrieved. If you woke up this morning and had no future, what do you think would be on your mind? You might be tempted to think that, with the future unavailable, you would turn to the present and past.

While this seems logical to those of us living fully, something else takes place first—or simultaneously—for those who are dying. Listen to their comments: "I won't get to walk my daughter down the aisle," said one patient. "I wonder what my grandchildren would have been like," said a mother of three whose children were still in their teens. "No more family gatherings at Thanksgiving," said another. "I had planned to go back to school after the kids left home. I so wanted to be a nurse. I won't get to do that now," said a forty-nine-year-old woman. What are all of these patients expressing? They are expressing what we the living think is reserved for those who survive the loss of a loved one: grief. The dying not only live in the past and present, but most actively grieve the loss of what they anticipated their future would hold for them. This knowledge can be very helpful for the caregiver, who most likely has no idea what is causing the deep sadness expressed by many patients. Caregivers have told me they assume the sadness has to do with the fact their patients are dying but never thought the dying were also grieving. What is true for the caregiver is also true of the dying person. Many do not know they are grieving, partly because grief is still not a widely acknowledged or discussed issue in our culture; this impedes an understanding of how grief manifests itself emotionally.

NO MORE

All change includes loss. When we leave home to enter college, we may be very happy to be moving forward with our lives, but loss is still present. We are no longer totally under our parents' care but living in an in-between place, between parental control and full responsibility for ourselves. In *Young Man Luther*, Erik Erikson called attending college a necessary period of "moratorium," a time-limited period that aids people in moving from one status to another. We are no longer in the status we were in; and many of us grieve the loss entailed in growing up, even as we look forward to and celebrate our new freedom. When we change jobs, get divorced, move to a new place, or get married, our status changes. It surprises some of us that inmates who have spent many years in prison are not happy to be released. Many find it hard to cope with their new freedom and responsibilities. Implicit in change, good or bad, is the loss of what was.

Brides and grooms also experience this, another surprise for many people. Their tears do not come because, as many suspect, they are unsure of their love for one another, but because in choosing *only* each other, they have inadvertently chosen to close off other relationship options *forever* and to end life in the single world, an entirely different world from the married one.

It would help people immensely who mistake their sadness prior to wedding ceremonies for doubt about their feelings of love to know that what they are feeling is grief for the losses that will accompany the moment of transition, the change from being single to being married. That moment is one of extreme joy and a moment of permanent *no mores*. No more being responsible for only me.

No more playing the field. No more independent decision-making. No more single-mindedness. *No more single future!* Marriage signals a new kind of freedom for many brides and grooms, but it also signals the end of freedom as they have known and experienced it. The end of single freedom is socially acknowledged in the ritual of the bachelor parties that precede weddings, but I wonder how many people today understand that this last fling is also a grief party. There is always a cost to change, and this entails grief.

We naturally assign grief to those whose futures will change because of a loss. When we see family and friends surrounding the bed of their loved one who is dying, we see their tears and feel their pain. We feel sad with them and do our best to accompany them through their grief journey, from anticipatory grief to the moment of death and after. For caregivers the natural focus is on the survivor. We must also know that those who are dying are also grieving. *No future* means *no more* of something or someone. *No more* isn't about the past, which the dying still have, but about the future that will no longer be. All of the *no mores* unfold in the dying person's mind as losses to be mourned. When I ask students what they think the dying will lose, they are quick to answer, "Everything." Yet, to say *everything* is to avoid *each thing,* each particular person, place, event, and dream that embraces, engages, and embodies our lives.

Facing the specific losses of the dying means facing our own losses, and we are not ready to do that. When I insist on fleshing out the word *everything*, the specifics come forth: While family, friends, and lovers—the survivors—will each lose one person and have to say goodbye to one person, the dying person will *lose each one* of them and must say goodbye to each one of them. How do they do this? How do the dying look at the sister, brother, parent, partner, friend, child, and colleague, who surround their sickbed, knowing that in a few short weeks or months they will no longer see them again, no longer experience their love, no longer share thoughts with them or enjoy their company, no longer see their accomplishments, their growth, and their achievements, and no longer be accompanied by them in life?

———◄o►———

I first learned about the dying person's need to grieve from one of my patients. Betty had been a nurse for twenty years. She was married, with one daughter. She had requested that her hospital bed be placed in the den so that she could receive visitors and be part of the daily life "downstairs." One day while I was visiting with her, she was distant and inattentive. Her eyes were looking somewhere else. At first, I tried to follow her gaze to see what occupied her, but was unable to locate the object of her attention. Nothing unusual was happening to distract her. Finally I asked her, "Betty, what are you looking at?" With tears in her eyes and sadness in her quivering voice, she answered, "At my dog." There, sitting

by the sliding glass doors in the den, and looking out the window, was Dolly, Betty's dog. "I'm
going to miss my little Dolly," she continued. For
the next thirty minutes, Betty told me when,
where, and under what circumstances she had
acquired Dolly, how Dolly got her name, what
a good friend and companion Dolly was, how
Dolly had been dealing with her illness, her concern about how Dolly would survive her death,
and how she would be cared for and by whom.

Betty was grieving. She had to mourn the
loss of her future with Dolly and of being in
control of Dolly's daily life after her death. She
had to come to terms with *no more*. Betty was
also aware of her need to grieve over the loss of
being a part of her daughter's life. Her daugh-

ter, Sammie, had just finished college and was about to embark on graduate studies. "My Sammie is a serious student. I wonder what she will finally decide on as a career," Betty began, "and I wonder if she will find love in her life, or if she will decide to have children. I will miss seeing my grandchildren if she has them, miss knowing their characters and personalities, how they will choose to live. I will miss that they will never know me." Tears streamed down Betty's cheeks as she expressed a need to tell her daughter her thoughts. Betty asked me to help facilitate their encounter. When I approached Sammie in the kitchen, she too expressed love for her mother, deep sadness and grief over her imminent death, and emptiness related to having to go on living without her mother in her life. She eagerly agreed to the meeting with her mother.

Sammie approached her mother's bed, gave her a kiss on the forehead, and took her hand. Without any prompting on my part, Betty began: "Sammie, I remember the day you were born. I was so excited, I couldn't wait to hold you and look into your eyes. You are the blessing of my life. As I look into your eyes now, I am so proud of you." Sammie began to cry and, slouching down to be as close to her mother as possible, said in turn, "I've always been proud that you were my mom, too. I want to thank you for my character, which I think comes from you, and for supporting me through everything. I love you." Betty and Sammie continued to talk about the past and about the future in which each one would miss the other. Somewhere in the middle of their conversation, I slipped out the door, realizing that I was now standing on sacred ground, listening to words that belonged only to their world.

———◆———

Betty, like other dying patients, had scores of people that she loved and whose loss she needed to grieve. Betty had sisters, a brother, nieces, nephews, cousins, parents, aunts and uncles, friends and colleagues, and people in her church community, all people whose lives she would no longer be a part of and whose futures she would no longer know about. We know of persons with AIDS who have lost lovers and hundreds of friends to the disease, and of Holocaust survivors who have lost hundreds of family members and their whole communities to the death camps of Europe. We never think of the dying person as a person who has multiple losses.

We think of the dying as someone else's loss. The dying say goodbye to those they love—those who will go on without them. It can be an overwhelming and exhausting task. At the same time, they must cope with futures they know they will never experience—more losses to grieve. Dying people express grief over having to leave their homes, the careers they will no longer be involved in, the car that was so important to have and cost so much, the investment risks for which they will not see results, and all of the unfulfilled dreams they still thought there was time to realize. One woman said to me that she would miss the sun, the ocean waves, the blue sky, and the planet.

Grieving the loss of the future, the *no mores* in life, the no more tomorrow, is an unavoidable, painful, and exhausting task for the dying person.

CHAPTER 4

HOPE AND LIFE REVIEW

BECAUSE WE LIVE in the world of the living and are working with people who are dying, we become a bridge from past patients, and the many lessons they have taught us, to patients we now serve. Because the dying have never died before—just as we have not—they do not know what to expect or know if what they are experiencing is normal. The power we hold with our patients is our ability to share with them words, stories, and experiences from the only ones who have the authority to help them, our previous patients from whom we learned. What the dying teach us will be multidimensional and many-leveled. Some of the learning will be from our own mistakes and successes as their caregivers. It is for us to keep in our hearts and in our journals their stories, their struggles, their victories and failures, and our own victories and failures in caring for them, and to pass them on to our patients and families as spiritual food.

Up to now, all may seem only doom for the person who hits the brick wall. Seeing their end in sight, realizing there is no more future as they knew it before, and grieving the loss of absolutely everything, including the loss of their own body, can be overwhelming. Of what benefit then is it to know that you are going to die? Isn't it better to simply die suddenly and avoid all this pain? At the same time that the shock of having hit the brick wall occurs, something else, something amazing, something deeply life-transforming is also taking place.

LIFE REVIEW

We live life forward and understand it backward.

—Søren Kierkegaard

The unexamined life is not worth living.

—Socrates

Life review is a term coined by Robert Butler in 1963 for the life-transforming process that occurs for the dying. According to Butler, life review "is a naturally occurring, universal mental process characterized by the progressive return to consciousness of past experiences, and, particularly, the resurgence of unresolved conflicts; simultaneously, and normally, these revived experiences and conflicts can be surveyed and reintegrated."[4]

Life review for the dying person, however, is quite different from life review for a person who has a future. Life review in the world of the living is a means of evaluating a specific part of the past or a specific time period. Sometimes we look back in order to go forward. We can enter into a life review whenever we choose to, as when we are enduring changes in our lives, like a divorce or a change of jobs. We also do life review when we are forced to look into the past because of a tragedy, whether it is a personal loss or a national tragedy like September 11. We look back to see where we have been, to evaluate our goals, and to then move into a new direction. Life review does not occupy our every moment. It is natural, but not automatic. We can stop it. We can refuse to look back. Sometimes, life review is sentimental, such as when we look over photo albums or videos of happy times now gone. We do reviews at socially designated times of the year, such as Thanksgiving and New Year's Eve. We watch movies that attempt to show us the benefits of reviewing our lives. *A Christmas Carol* and *It's a Wonderful Life* are two such movies.

They are repeated on television during the season of Christmas and New Year's to inspire spiritual renewal. The main character in each movie enters, albeit reluctantly, into an honest *look back* over his life, a task and a journey that ultimately leads to a deep and joyful renewal of life for each man.

When people hit a brick wall and no longer have a future, they no longer have the choice to look forward. The future simply isn't there as it was *before*. Unlimited vision is the illusive domain reserved only for the living. A dying person may look to the future of someone else—her children or grandchildren—caring deeply that they may be happy and well. The person may imagine what will be for others or for the world, but they no longer can plan or project themselves into the future of those lives, because they will not be there. They cannot dwell very long in a place where they will never exist, in the future of others. When a person can no longer look forward because there is no place to look, they look back. In the world of the living, we can *choose* to look back over our lives. In the world of the dying, the dying person has no choice. They now have a tiny, or short, future, but the quality and nature of this little future differ from the future they once had as a person who was always living with five more years to live.

In the world of the dying, life review appears to have three characteristics. It is automatic; it is nonselective; and it needs to be completed before a person dies. Is it true in every case? We cannot know. But it is true in enough cases to warrant our attention.

LIFE REVIEW: AUTOMATIC

For the dying, life review is *automatic*. They cannot refuse to look back. With the heartfelt lifelong assumption broken that there is endless time ahead, the dying have the strange experience of distancing the self from real time. The brick wall blocking their view of the future now takes the form of a tombstone—a tombstone that has both dates on it, birth date and death year. A terminal prognosis means that instead of life going forward, it is now the end of acquiring experiences a person seeks when well; it is time to look back at a whole life lived from the vantage point of the end and to look for a summary.

———◄◦►———

As a pastime, my parents love to drive through cemeteries looking at tombstones. While they do not understand my working with the dying and refuse any discussion of the subject of death, they frequently make inadvertent observations that are insightful about the experience of dying or death. One day my mother called me to tell me that during one of their cemetery tours she noticed an epitaph on a young man's tombstone that she thought would interest me. The epitaph was not a statement, as one might expect, but a question: "What was that all about?" I laughed when I heard it. "What was that all about?" We do not know what prompted this epitaph, but it fascinated me that it was on a tombstone memorializing a man in his thirties. Some tombstones are witticisms specified in the deceased's will. Other times words such as "We will love you always" are written by relatives or friends. This question, because it was on a tombstone, immediately made me think that the decedent must have had time to think about and prepare for his death, and that the question must have been on his lips often enough for him to be memorialized in such a way. Maybe it was the question asked in the life review of the dying, "What was *my life* [that] all about?"

———◄◦►———

At the end of life, people ask existential questions, sometimes for the first time. *Was I put on earth for a specific purpose? Did I live out that purpose? What meaning did my life have? Who did I love? Who loved me? What kind of person was I? Was I kind, loving, and approachable? Did I ignore people or treat them badly? What accomplishments did I make? What achievements did I attain? What regrets do I have? What dreams did I live out and which dreams are lost forever? Will I be remembered? Did I make a difference?* The questions go on and on as each person evaluates and summarizes the difference they made or did not make for having lived.

LIFE REVIEW: NONSELECTIVE

Life review for the dying is *nonselective*. I may, in the world of the living, choose to reminisce by looking back over photos of my college years. I may also be thrown into the past by a smell, a scene in a movie, or by any number of sensory triggers. I may also choose not to dwell there very long, especially if the memory is a bad one or if I need to get on with the present, a present which is determined by my future goals and dreams that are still waiting to be actualized.

A person who is dying cannot avoid, block, or shut off life review. Reawakened memories come forward without a conscious decision— everything from the smallest indiscretions and accomplishments to the greatest events that had been blocked from memory or had been forgotten. Life review takes place during waking hours, sleeping hours, and in unconscious states. *Nonselective* means everything is going to come flooding back, in whatever order, unedited, without priori-

tization or censorship of any sort, as illustrated by
the story that follows.

The husband of one patient noted that his wife
was mumbling through the night, naming and
talking to familiar people at an event that he
remembered had taken place forty years earlier. "Why was she there?" he asked. When the
patient and I spoke about her reminiscence, she
confided that it was at this event that she had
had an opportunity to have a relationship with
another man. She recalled the subtle flirting and
the genuine caring emotions that rippled deeply
between them. And she remembered the slow,
awkward turning away from him as a decision

not to pursue her feelings. "In my heart," she said, "I knew this could have been the love I had always longed for. But I chose to remain faithful to my husband. I wonder now how my life might have been different had I gone through with it. I was afraid to take the risk, but I also felt obligated to my prior choice. I think I did the right thing."

LIFE REVIEW:
COMPLETED BEFORE DEATH

Dying persons are compelled to complete their life review before dying. One's entire life must finally be summarized and evaluated, and come to a close. "What was *that* all about?" has to be answered. But it has to be answered with satisfaction. Those of us who have worked with dying patients have at times witnessed the patient who should have died days earlier but kept hanging on. With a barely audible heartbeat, and without water or food for days, the patient has *decided* not to die yet. When we can determine that they are not waiting for a loved one to visit, or a special day or event to pass, we sometimes can assess that the patient's life review is left wanting. The patient isn't satisfied with the outcome. And the patient will not let go until she deems her life *ready*. Something within human nature seems to seek wholeness, and persons want to die whole, or complete.

—◄○►—

A young married man with three teenagers was dying. Two days before his death, he started to clean every room in the house in a meticulous, energetic, but calm manner. He started in his and his wife's bedroom, emptying every drawer and closet, returning items in a folded and orderly fashion. This took hours. He then proceeded to his children's three bedrooms, the living room, dining room, family room, kitchen, basement, and garage, meticulously unpacking, cleaning, folding, shelving, throwing out, and finally placing everything back. His wife called the hospice, frantic. "He's driving us crazy," she said, "and he isn't talking at all. Can't you give him something to stop him?" The hospice team met, and it didn't take us long to figure out what was going on. Our patient, George, was acting out, externally, his inner journey. Whatever he was reviewing, he needed to finalize. We surmised he was "putting his house in order." And sure enough, when George completed a marathon twenty-four hours of cleaning the inside of every possible cubbyhole and drawer in the house, he lay down and a day later died.

Sometimes, especially when time is very short, the patient cannot be successful in pursuing their life review. If they do not have the verbal ability, it is impossible for us to discover what is left unresolved. The patient is left, often in a nonresponsive state, to deal with it themselves before they die.

THE GIFT OF LIFE REVIEW

Often, life review prompts that patient to set a spiritual agenda for the tiny future left, before allowing death to come. This is the gift of life review.

At the end of life, life review cannot be avoided. Life review happens automatically. It entails looking back over one's entire life: a holy entanglement of many threads that requires sorting through, deep reflection, summarization, and sometimes decisions. For example, when a particular scene or event relentlessly repeats itself, it signals that something is unresolved. The patient becomes *stuck* and cannot move forward until the impasse is resolved.

Life review is a gift because it brings the possibility of growth and real change at the end of life. How do we grow and create change in our lives? If we are honest with ourselves, some life tasks are just too risky for us to undertake. Changing parts of ourselves that we think need to be changed, or that need to be changed though we don't know it, is a task many avoid. Change and growth are hard because what we want to alter is not a behavior that occurs only once but an established pattern in our thinking and behavior.

Have you ever had someone say to you, "You *always* . . ." We often deny such comments, becoming defensive. "I do not *always*," we hear ourselves saying. Yet, even if we are aware of our patterns, the question still remains: How do we change what is deeply and habitually ingrained? How do we change what is the only way we have ever been and the only way we know how to be?

Sometimes a pattern can be acknowledged and changed during our life journey, such as when people recognize they are alcoholics or that they are serial spousal abusers, or that they marry and divorce the same kind of person time and time again. What isn't completed in our personal journey during our lifetime often appears as final tasks to accomplish at the end of life. Elisabeth Kübler-Ross noted, "We all have lessons to learn during this time called life; this is especially apparent when working with the dying. The dying learn a great deal at the end of life, usually when it is too late to apply." In my own experience, and in the experience of many hospice workers, the dying bear out this truth. It is not uncommon for a hospice nurse to approach other team members, such as the social worker or chaplain, and tell us that by all clinical diagnoses, the patient should not be alive.

Kübler-Ross stated why she thought she did not die after having a stroke in 1995: "But I have not died because I am still learning the lessons of life, my final lessons. These lessons are the ultimate truths about our lives. ... When we have passed the tests we were sent to earth to learn, we are allowed to graduate. We are allowed to shed our body."[5]

These tests, or lessons, are often about our established patterns of thinking and behavior, what we often hear referred to as "just who you are."

SPIRITUALITY AND PATTERNS

In Judaism, *chazakah* (a presumption of fact) of a person's character is determined when a person repeats an act, whether good or bad, three times. At three, it is considered a firmly established way of being, a *chazakah*. Remember, *most* criminals are not in jail because they did something once but because they finally got caught. The repeated act is no longer something that the person does. He becomes what he repeats. What he repeats becomes identified with his character, and until he changes himself through repentance, it stays part of him. In spite of this, Judaism teaches that every person, no matter how sinful, can always change his behavior and character through sincere repentance (*teshuvah*).

Paul was a patient with a six-month prognosis who was now entering his ninth month of hospice home care. He was a rough, arrogant, self-centered, independent, and egocentric man. He only allowed the nurse to visit him. He refused visits from all other members of the hospice team, which included the social worker, chaplain, and volunteer. One day, unexpectedly, he asked the nurse to "have that chaplain" visit. I scheduled the visit.

When I arrived, Paul's wife answered the door. I introduced myself and was greeted with a suspicious look and a stern voice: "I don't know what he wants to see you for, but when you see him, don't tell him he's dying. He doesn't know." I mused at how often I had been the recipient of this same command of deception, which was a clear indication of the closed communication between the patient and others, resulting in loneliness for all parties. She ushered me into the bedroom, where Paul lay still on his back, staring at a picture of Jesus on the wall. The door closed behind me, leaving Paul and me alone. Paul neither said hello nor offered me a seat. I sat down quietly in the wooden chair next to his bed. Paul continued to stare at the picture of Jesus, seemingly unaffected by my presence. Finally, Paul broke the silence. "I've been thinking about my life," he said. I will never forget this opening sentence, these ordinary words, this preface that would define the place from which Paul's thoughts would emerge. These words characterize the essence of his and every dying person's task, the requirement to look back. What Paul didn't know was that he had no choice in the matter.

"I've been thinking about my life," he said. *Of course,* I heard my inner voice gently and silently acknowledge. Hadn't Paul been doing that for the past nine months? Why had he waited until now to talk about it? I waited to hear what would come next. He continued. "When I was a young child, my mother died. My older sister raised me. I have to hand it to her. It wasn't an easy job, but she did it and did it well. I never thanked her. I never told her how much I appreciated her efforts. Actually, I don't have much of a relationship with my sister at all. Never did once I grew up."

Paul paused, and then he shifted his thoughts from his sister to his work. "For forty years I worked on Wall Street. In the beginning, my colleagues used to ask me to eat lunch with them and wanted to get together with our wives on weekends. I always refused. I was self-absorbed, not interested in anything but doing my job and making money. I had my own goals. I refused the friendliness of others."

Paul paused again before shifting his thoughts to his third and final subject. "My marriage isn't good. I've been married for forty-five years. Never told my wife I loved her. Didn't do things with her or for her. Most weekends she went out with her girlfriends to movies and dinner. I figured I worked hard all week and deserved to do what I wanted to do on weekends. I mostly sat in my chair and read and slept. I wanted to be alone. I wanted to rest." Paul paused again and then pondered aloud incredulously, "I can't believe how wonderfully my wife has taken care of me at home since I've been sick. She's done such a good job."

Paul was finished. He turned his head toward me, looking into my eyes for the first time.

He then uttered the question that prompted him to request my presence in the first place, a question that could only follow his threefold confession of sorts, a question that, if answered, might lead him out of the spiritual quicksand that threatened to devour him before his bodily death. So this was the meaning of the visit! The question was simple, sincere, and as ordinary and benign as his opening words. "Can you help?" he asked, his tone sounding as if he had never before in his life asked for anything. "Can you help?" he asked and I could see in his moist eyes a quiet desperation. A silence followed, filled for Paul with the hope of a direction, a course of action, or a word that might free him in some way that had totally eluded him.

I had a choice. I could use the Rogerian technique, as I learned in pastoral care classes, whereby you put the patient's words back to him in the form of a question. "So, you need help? What kind of help do you think you need?" Had Paul asked me this question in the early weeks of his illness, I no doubt would have heard the question differently than I heard it in his ninth month of illness. Beware of employing *technique* instead of discerning how to be human in a situation. Sometimes technique is helpful for clarification, to help the patient explore in more depth what she is looking for or why she feels she needs help, to explore the options she thought were available to her, or simply to give the interviewer a moment of respite to think. Because I was familiar with Paul's case through interdisciplinary team meetings, and because he had outlived his prognosis by months and should have already died, I sensed in Paul a man who had no idea how to proceed.

I could also do what clergy have since told me I should have done—heard his message as a confession and given him absolution to allow him to die with a peaceful heart. After all, Paul was Catholic. It would be the Christian thing to do.

INNER DIALOGUE

My mind was working fast. I wasn't sure what I was going to say or do. Stuff zoomed into my mind as sweat beaded up on my neck. *My role as a chaplain*, I told myself, *is not to take away the pain of another person, although some people think it is. I could ask him to look at another part of his life review to see his accomplishments, to see that he isn't as bad a person as he thinks he is. No, that would be leading. That would be my agenda. That would be me wanting him to feel better about himself. This is not what Paul is saying. It has taken nine months of reminiscing and sifting through the past for Paul to discover the patterns of his thinking and behavior that he thinks cheated him of a better life. It has taken Paul three months past his expected death date to realize that he is holding on to life because he does not want to die the man he lived. He can cheat death only so long, and the extension he has given himself so far has not reaped the resolve he thought he could come to by himself. After all, he has always depended on only his own inner resources to move forward in life. These resources have failed him now. Paul is stuck, really stuck. And he is dying. He can't hold death off much longer. Having reached his limits, he is compelled—even forced—to invite me, a stranger into his house, a stranger whom he now trusts will take his pain seriously and not treat his accounts as anything less than a dead man's final plea for life.*

Don't think of this as a plea for forgiveness. Paul did not mention forgiveness, or God. Stay with his pain as Elihu stayed with Job in his pain. That's your job—that and to acknowledge that his pain is real and valid. Don't whisk it away with forgiveness. Don't be tempted to smooth over his pain by using his life review to recount his accomplishments. What does he want from me? Something he isn't aware of himself. His only chance is that I will get it right.

PATTERNS, PATTERNS, PATTERNS

Paul had not clearly defined his problem, but his three stories revealed the problem as his *pattern of relating*. What we need to change in our lives, in large part, does not concern one-time actions or thoughts but rather repeated patterns of thinking and doing that hurt others or interfere and block our ability to live fully. Paul was distressed because the only way he knew how to relate to others, his pattern, was so deeply ingrained that he was immobilized and unable to see how to relate in any other way. He did not know what to do. He couldn't free himself from these habitual patterns. He was stuck. Nine months of life review had revealed a pattern of thinking and behaving so deeply ingrained in Paul that it was *normal* to him. It was Paul's *normal* that needed redeeming, Paul's *normal* that was all he was left with in his desert experience.

So when Paul so blatantly asked for help, I responded, "Is your sister still living? Are your co-workers still living in the neighborhood? Can you tell your wife what you told me about your marriage and your appreciation for her caring for you? Can you tell them what you've told me?"

"Don't you think he knew to do that?" someone asked me. No! What is apparent to us as outsiders is not apparent to the person inside the pattern. Paul had one pattern of relational behavior. He did not know how to put one foot in front of the other any differently than he always had done. I suggested a new pattern of relating to others for Paul to consider, one of honest discourse and encounter. Without further conversation, questioning, or arguing, Paul's only response was "Thanks." Without knowing the outcome of this final journey with loved ones and friends, or even if he would live long enough to see me, he gave himself a week and arranged one last meeting with me: "Come back next week."

BEFORE WE GET TO THE ENDING: ARCHETYPES

I pause here to clarify what is taking place in Paul, as one of many archetypal journeys our patients may embark on at the end of life. It behooves us to learn more about the journeys we embark on as human beings, so that we can be of help to our patients as they pursue their spiritual tasks. Paul's journey is but one of several archetypal journeys that could be discerned.

Archetypes are a spiritual tool for deciphering a patient's spiritual journey (and ours). According to Carl Jung, archetypes are "primordial images common to humanity." This means that they are common patterns of human experience, what we might call inborn tendencies of the psyche, or psychic structures. It is important to note that these structures, tendencies, or common patterns are *empty of content,* just as the universal framework I am offering you is empty of content, or Kübler-Ross's grief stages are empty of content. It is the personal life and journey of the individual that fills the emptiness with content. As humans, we are predisposed to certain archetypal—or common—themes and images that come alive in us when we are prompted by certain events.

BEFORE WE GET TO THE ENDING: INDIVIDUATION

One such archetypal theme is *individuation*. It is Jung who asserts that all human beings are predisposed to become what they are meant to be. For Jung, this is a natural process of growth. Marked by crises or brick wall events, individuation is a process whereby a person slowly becomes conscious of the self and learns to live out who he or she really is. We see this journey in the biblical figure of Jacob as he journeys from an ego-centered and cheating person to a loving, honest, and other-centered person. His journey is so complete, his essence so altered, that he is given a new name, Israel, as a sign that he is a new person. For Jung, individuation is the journey toward wholeness, a journey that is widely seen among hospice caregivers of varying religious and nonreligious persuasions as the innate goal of patients at the end of life.

BEFORE WE GET TO THE ENDING: A JEWISH PERSPECTIVE ON THE PARABLE OF THE PRODIGAL SON (LIFE REVIEW AND REPENTANCE)

Individuation resulting from a brick wall event, as well as a new interpretation of the experience of the younger son in the parable of the Prodigal Son (in Luke 15), helped me to understand Paul's change of heart, based on his life review, as an archetypal journey toward wholeness that many patients encounter at the end of life. The story of the Prodigal Son also helped me to understand the spiritual significance of life review and its relationship to the religious concept of repentance.

It is widely debated among Christian scholars whether the parable of the Prodigal Son (sometimes called the Waiting Father) is about repentance. My own recollection of sermons and commentaries is that the younger son—who shamefully asks his father for his half of the inheritance, gets it, and squanders it in partying—does not want to return home because he is sorry but because he is the narcissistic brat he was in the first place, albeit now in dire straits.

When I ask Christian audiences what parable they dislike the most—actually I say *hate*—it is this one, and one other we will see later. Not only do they see the returning younger son as a brat, but they also see the father as "a naïve chump," as one man put it. He added, "I feel a bit guilty saying so though, since I know that the father in the story represents God." What lesson they are to learn from the parable is confusing. Repentance seems inauthentic—forgiveness a sham.

I think that the reason for the confusion has to do with the fact that after the destruction of the Second Temple in 70 CE[6] and Christianity's subsequent separation from Judaism, Christian interpretations permeated the parables. Since the Holocaust, there has been a surge of scholarly interest, both Christian and Jewish, into the theology of Jesus the Jew. The Jewish period in which Jesus lived is known as the Second Temple Period.

It was at a conference in Jerusalem that I received an explanation of this parable from a Jewish perspective. I was living in Israel at the time (1998–2000), at a post-Holocaust Christian moshav (an agricultural collective) called Nes Ammim (meaning, in Hebrew, "a sign to the nations"). The community itself was founded as a Christian response of repentance and renewal toward the Jewish people for the murder of six million Jews in predominantly Christian European countries during the Second World War. Because repentance was inherent to the founding, purpose, and idea of Nes Ammim, I was asked to give the opening presentation on Christian repentance at a conference by the Interreligious Coordinating Council in Israel, in Jerusalem. Christian and Jewish clergy and members of religious orders were participants.

I chose this parable as a way of beginning. I realized some of the rabbis at the conference had been born in Israel and were therefore *not* likely to know much about Christianity or its scriptural texts; therefore they had not experienced Christian anti-Semitism except through history and would have a fresh perspective on the text. Was it about repentance? Was it Jewish in its understanding? It was the only text I could think of to offer that might have something to do with repentance. I simply lifted the parable from the New Testament, placed it on plain paper—with no mention of Jesus or God—just a story about a father and two sons. I asked participants to tell me what they thought the story was about.

Most of the Christians who knew the story well said it was about the father who forgives unconditionally. One Israeli rabbi, however, said, "Clearly this story is about repentance—*teshuvah*—and it is clearly a Jewish parable." I asked if he knew this parable already. He said no. "Really?" I said. "How can you tell it is a Jewish parable, and what makes you think it is about repentance?" His answer was both revelatory and humorous. "The parable is a method used by rabbis to teach a message through familiar and ordinary stories. It has something to say to all levels of people, and it seizes the spiritual fiber of the heart. Parables show God's nature in human life, and how God wants us to treat each other." Then he added with a smile, "It's also evident that it's a Jewish parable because it is about a father and two sons. We talk a lot about fathers with two sons." He smiled. We laughed. Cain and Abel, Jacob and Esau, Isaac and Ishmael, and more filled our minds. He continued, "The writer of this parable was a rabbi and knew of other rabbinic parables, oral or written, as resources."

Then he stated emphatically, "This parable is about repentance." I was surprised at his comments. I thought, *Jesus had rabbinic sources for his parables? He can tell this is a Jewish story? It's clearly about repentance?* The rabbi then told other rabbinic parables about repentance that had the same theological themes: a son leaving home for a far country; a father waiting for his return; the son "coming to himself"; the shame of the son who does not know how to return; and the welcome of the father who meets him partway.

The next day he gave us a rabbinic parable with the same imagery and theme.

> Return, O Israel, unto the Lord thy God. Consider the parable of a prince who was far away from his father— a hundred days' journey away. His friends said to him: "Return to your fa-

ther." He replied: "I cannot: I have not the strength." Thereupon his father sent word, saying to him: "Come back as far as you can according to your strength, and I will go the rest of the way to meet you." So the Holy One, blessed be He, says to Israel: Return unto Me, and I will return unto you. (MAL. 3:7)[7]

Then he interpreted the parable as conveying the *first* step in repentance from a Jewish perspective and of God's response of mercy to a repentant sinner. "In Judaism," he said, "all you need is to have a heartfelt desire to change as the very first thing, and God will come to meet you and help you the rest of the way. The rest of the way has steps to it—like really changing and not repeating the sin in the future [these steps will be presented in another section later]—but this parable is clearly about a young man's changed heart. The text says, 'He came to himself.' In early Judaism, at least, poverty could cause a person, who beforehand had everything, to recognize his need for God. It brings him to consciousness. We see God then, eager to respond with mercy and forgiveness to a person who truly repents." In contrast, many a Christian sees the poverty of the young man not as something that brings him to recognize God but as a survival issue. He returns to his father because he is hungry.

In Judaism, a change of heart is the beginning of *teshuvah,* which is a long and arduous process. (Just think of how sincerely we all make New Year's resolutions and how easily we fail to live up to them. This kind of thing is not *teshuvah*.) In Judaism it is fundamentally the person *who does the work* to alter their own behavior, while God responds with love and mercy *to provide the strength* to change. In contrast, traditional Christian understanding of the text focuses on the forgiving father as Jesus, as the one *who does the work* of atoning for the son's sin, who takes the son's shame upon himself; this is a Christological and not Jewish interpretation, hence the confusion in the minds of so many Christians as to the meaning of the parable.

Jesus, who told this parable, did so from the education he received in a rabbinic environment and culture, with the idea that the young man's poverty brought him to a consciousness of his sin and, in "coming to himself," a desire to go home.

When I had my last visit with Paul, all this came flashing back; individuation—the journey toward wholeness, repentance—the change of heart, the desire for something new and wholesome. Paul's life review and desire for help also helped me to see the parable all the more clearly.

Paul had a deep desire to change. He was aware of his destructive pattern of relating to others. His heart was open to do something about it. "Can you help?" he asked, but he did not know to turn around, how to travel in a new direction; and he did not know where it would lead. In faith, he simply started the journey.

It is with Paul that I discovered *life review* is a kind of secular form of the religious idea of repentance. In looking back, in evaluating honestly, in recognizing one's destructive or hurtful acts or patterns of relating, one can opt to change. Life review can bring consciousness and a deep desire to change. Paul's next step, like that of the Prodigal Son, was "to come to himself." Out of his life review, Paul began the journey home, choosing wholesome yet difficult action, without knowing where the journey would end.

———◦———

When I left Paul, he asked me to "come back" the next week, which I did. His wife once again greeted me at the front door. "I don't know what you talked about last week," she said, "but a stream of people has been visiting him every day all week, including my sister, whom he has hated. He hasn't let me come into his room for any of these visits, so I don't know what has been going on. All I know is that everyone has come out crying." She told me that Paul had confronted her with their shared secret knowledge of his impending death, and that they cried together. She told me that he confessed his lack of caring for her in their marriage, that he loved her and thanked her for caring for him now. He had called the funeral director, priest, and lawyer, making plans for his funeral service and drafting a will. He had asked the children to come over and had given each of them some of their inheritance.

When I entered Paul's bedroom, he did not share any details of the previous week. He merely said, "I did what you said." There was a pause, and he added, "But I have one last regret."

"What is that?" I asked.

"I regret that I didn't live my whole life like this."

I was again aware that my first instinct was to take away Paul's pain, to assure him that he had done some good things in life, to recount his accomplishments and achievements. But I realized my need to relieve my own discomfort and his suffering by taking away his pain was not what Paul needed or was asking for. That would have been my agenda, not his. By attempting to take away his pain, I would have signified to Paul that in the past week he had not broken with his lifelong way of relating to others. It had taken Paul seventy-odd years to face his pain, to share it, and to ask for help. It was not my place to snatch that away from him and to deny him the only opportunity he had left at self-redemption.

Religious paradigms—Judaic, Christian, Buddhist—speak loudly on this scenario of being lost and then found, being dead and then alive, being enslaved but then liberated, being attached and then experiencing the joy of impermanence. Paul was lost. It was not my place to snatch away Paul's pain, for only by steeping himself in his pain could he experience its opposite. I did not want to cheat him for the sake of a false comfort. I was silent for a long moment.

"No, you did not live your life before the way you did this last week. Nothing can change that." This was an affirmation of his self-assessment (rather than what I was tempted to say: "Oh Paul, come on, you aren't as bad as you make out. I'm sure we can find times and events in your life where you helped people or made a difference.").

Then came a dawning, an epiphany. And as it came, I shared it with Paul. "It's just dawning on me, Paul, that in this last week you have discovered a new man inside yourself, one that you never met before, one that your family and friends have never met before. And it is this new man that is the gift that you give your family, friends, and yourself, before you die. Is that an accurate statement?" Paul's eyes widened in affirmation of this thought and then filled with tears of joy that could not be contained. Paul's essence had changed. He was no longer the man he had been. He was a new creation, one which neither he nor his family and friends nor I could have ever imagined existed.

I now understood why those who visited Paul in that last week left his room weeping. They wept because they had met a man in Paul whom they had never known before, and because they knew as they left his room that they would never see him again. This was a man they would have liked to know better. They were grieving. Paul had *really* changed, and he knew it. Paul had the desire and the courage to face the unknown and to step out of himself and to be what he had never been before. What Paul did in effect is what Judaism teaches as repentance.

Repentance is a word that conjures feelings of sorrow, joylessness, and heaviness. We don't think we will find new hope and deep everlasting joy. We don't leap at the chance to repent.

When I saw how Paul's life had changed by life review, I began to suspect that this nonreligious spiritual process of renewal paralleled the religious notion of repentance. I had never before seen repentance work like this. I had never witnessed repentance changing a person. It was the ordinary process of hitting a brick wall, followed spontaneously by the life review process, that gave life to the religious notion in ways I had not heretofore seen. Yet, when we look at Paul's story, we see repentance in action. *Repentance*, in the spiritual sense, means to turn around, to see things in a way you have never seen them before, to become a new person.

The rabbis in Jerusalem had spoken of a whole process involved in repentance. Now, when I teach how change is effected, I use a personal example to illustrate that process, one that helps people remember.

I love pens. In fact, I lust after pens. I love their bodies the way some people love the bodies of cars. I love their curves and shapes, their thinness, their thickness, the way they feel when I write, their different colors, the different plastics or steel that pens are made of. I love the way pens feel in my fingers.

I recall an episode of *All in the Family* in which Archie Bunker defends the practice, which "everybody does," of taking home items from work and not considering it stealing. He mentions pens. Those who make pens also know how people love them. That's why they have created so many different types, shapes, colors, and textures of pens. We choose a pen for its ink quality, its smoothness, its wet or dry application, its fine or thick spread, and its body. We choose the pen that best suits our work position, or the pen that seems to parallel the seriousness or lack of seriousness of the project we are undertaking. We may choose a special pen for writing in our journals, or for impressing someone.

I know that I have pens in my possession that I did not borrow, that were not given to me as a gift, and that I did not buy. Yet, I never think of myself as having *stolen* any of them.

When I was packing to move home from Israel in 2000, I was aware that the cost of shipping my belongings home was by the pound. I was therefore selective as to what I packed. As I cleaned out desk drawers, briefcases, and purses, I was left with a pile of pens that must have numbered two hundred. "Two years worth of pens," I remember saying. I considered whether or not I should take them home, but decided against the extra weight. I gathered all the pens and took them back to the office. As my secretary watched me, I placed them in front of him on his desk. His eyes got big, his mouth gaping wide open in astonishment. "It was *you*," he said with an accusing tone. "It was *you*," he repeated in disbelief and anger. "I wondered where all the pens went. I kept ordering box after box and they kept disappearing." I remember feeling flushed and defensive. "What do you mean, 'It was *you*?' I brought them back, didn't I?" Huffing and puffing, I walked out of the office.

I began to think of all the pens over all the years that ended up in my possession that I never bought. When I borrow a pen, there is a part of me that *knows* that I will forget to give it back, that *knows* that in the distraction of everyone getting up and talking to each other as they leave, the person who lent me the pen will forget to ask for it back. I thought, too, how I hoped I would be able to go home with the pens I "borrowed."

I also began to visualize the pens I liked and the pens I didn't like, and I drifted back to my childhood love of pens. I recalled fondly how I would ask my parents for money every week to buy ink cartridges for my Sheaffer fountain pen. I remembered how important pens made me feel, how I held them, touched them, looked at them, and made them visible by placing them in a pocket, on my desk, or on my ear. I loved pens. They symbolized thoughts made visible. I recalled how I wanted to be a writer, a thinker—an essayist. That is what I answered my fifth grade teacher when she asked me what I wanted to be when I grew up. I had found Ralph Waldo Emerson's essays, and even though I could only understand a sentence or two here and there, I was sure that writing my thoughts was what I wanted to do. "An essayist," I responded, and the teacher was duly impressed. Pens held a symbolic lure for me.

One day I said it *only* to myself, and not aloud. Silently I acknowledged, *I steal pens!* I don't just borrow pens. My intention when I ask to borrow a pen is always to keep it, always to count on the other person forgetting they have lent it to me. I would rationalize: *But pens are replaceable and inexpensive. I never take pens that are given to someone as gifts or are expensive.*

Everyone has pens that don't belong to them, and how many times have people approached me and said, "Oh, I like that pen. Where did you get it? You'd better hold on to it or you'll find it missing." The lust for pens is openly admitted, I thought.

Admitting one's indiscretion to oneself is the first step in repentance. It isn't uttered aloud. It is an inner awareness. It is the voice of remorse surfacing.

I say it again, and this time I look in the mirror, look into my own eyes and say it. "Kathleen, you steal pens." Saying it aloud makes all the difference. We know how many secrets families keep, secrets that everyone knows about but no one dares say, because saying it aloud means the end of denial, the end of a tense peace, the end of escape. By saying it aloud to myself, I openly acknowledged it. I exposed it to the air. There was no taking it back. It was no longer a silent secret. Admitting something aloud to yourself is step two of repentance.

In step three of repentance, I confess my wrongdoing to the one I have wronged and, if possible, I compensate for my wrongdoing. If I borrowed (or stole) a pen from someone when I spoke at a conference and I see her the next year at another conference, I have an opportunity to give it back. I can say, "Remember last year when I was speaking to this group and forgot my pen? You lent me yours, and I never returned it. Actually, I really never borrowed it from you. My intention was to steal it, and I did. *I steal pens!*" Now, I could just return the pen without admitting that I stole it, but then I've admitted nothing: I've simply lied and said I borrowed it and forgot to return it. I haven't changed. For real change to take place, I must tell her that I didn't borrow the pen. On the pretense of borrowing, I stole it.

Returning the pen is step three, compensation, giving back what I have taken. If I've lost the pen I took from her, then I give her another pen of the same or better worth. This, however, is not the end of the process of repentance, although it may seem complete with compensation. I must now do something different.

I must not repeat the action of stealing pens. This step is called *desisting from sin*. I prefer to call it *don't repeat*.

One could be deceived into thinking that not repeating constitutes full repentance, but it doesn't. Repentance, in this case, is acceptable and may be as far as I can go, but it is not complete. If I'm an alcoholic, this step is as far as I can go, because I will always be an alcoholic. If I don't continue to steal pens, but I still lust after pens, at least by not repeating the act of stealing pens I no longer hurt other people. If I do not repeat stealing pens out of fear of getting caught or because I am afraid of God's punishment, this is *repentance rooted in fear.*

A higher form is *repentance rooted in love.* While the core of repentance is to desist from repeating, at its highest, repentance is when I no longer *desire* to steal pens. When I no longer desire to steal pens, the essence of my being has changed. That is step five. In Judaism, this is called *repentance of purification*, when the very essence of a person changes. This repentance is what concerns us here with the dying, with Paul.

CHANGING NEGATIVE PATTERNS
IN BUDDHISM

Buddhists also speak of repeated negative patterns, mental states, or difficult energies of the mind and how to overcome them. These are sensory desire, anger, boredom, restlessness, and doubt. These five hindrances are so called because they thwart spiritual growth in the person.

Buddhism does not accept suppressing desires as an antidote. Suppression lasts only a moment and is usually implemented at the very moment the hindering pattern emerges and causes pain. Instead, elimination of hindrances must first come, as in Judaism, through desiring to be rid of them. Buddhism stresses observing how and when each obstacle emerges or appears and discovering positive forces to defeat them.

Portia Nelson's poem "Autobiography in Five Short Chapters" is often quoted by Buddhists in the context of facing and conquering negative patterns. I first read her poem in Sogyal Rinpoche's book *The Tibetan Book of Living and Dying*.

Nelson's poem begins with the realization that you are in a negative situation.

"I walk down the street. There is a hole in the sidewalk. I fall in." Of course, you don't know how you got there. It isn't a pattern yet.

She then tells how long it takes and how hard it is to get out.

I think about how many of us never leave a bad marriage, or a destructive job, or stop drinking. It takes luck or courage to get out. For how few!

The next three stanzas (chapters) begin the same: "I walk down the same street. There is a deep hole in the sidewalk." Chapter two still isn't a pattern. It takes three to make a pattern. But in chapter two, you realize you've been there before, and you don't want to be there again. If you are lucky or courageous, you get out.

Chapter three (stanza three) starts the same but continues differently: "I walk down the same street. There is a deep hole in the sidewalk." I like to say it my way. Heck! You jump in. It's your hole! What else? You now see it's a pattern, a way of life, no other option. You recognize it as such once you are in the hole, and you get out—quick! Whew! This is if you have the luck, courage, fortitude, and desire needed to go forward in search of wholeness.

Chapter four, fourth stanza, is simple enough. Transition time. "I walk down the same street. There is a deep hole in the sidewalk." What do you do next? You don't jump in. You walk around it. Here, we see the "no repeating" in Buddhism as well as in Jewish repentance. It's when the alcoholic stops drinking but is still an alcoholic. The hole is still there, tempting.

Chapter five. What can be different? What can bring wholeness and healing and a complete turning around? Repentance. "I walk down another street." What a journey! As Kübler-Ross would say, what a lesson to learn before you die. Just like Paul did.

What is significant for our conversation is that the Jewish or Buddhist way of overcoming negative patterns in life, far from being religiously obscure, or even boring, is borne out in the spiritual reality of those who are dying. Recognizing our negative patterns of behavior can result in a real desire to change. That change requires a courageous strategy of mind and heart, a spiritual strategy consisting of making amends and of planting and fostering new and positive thoughts and actions.

What Chögyam Trungpa Rinpoche says regarding our negative patterns may well be true for spiritual growth: "These difficulties are manure for *bodhi*, manure for awakening or enlightenment."[8] This was certainly true for Paul, and it can be for us too.

CHAPTER 5

Who Am I?

When I am speaking to an audience, I ask them this question: What was the first thing that you did this morning? When you got up, did you sit quietly at a table somewhere in your house, take paper and pen, and write the words "Who am I?" They laugh, because they know that this isn't the first or anywhere near the first or last thing they do in the morning or any other time during the day.

Most of the time, we live in the forgetfulness of being. Our morning routines confirm this, whatever they are. We get up, go to the bathroom, turn the coffee on, let the dogs out (or take them for a walk), read the paper, shower, eat, make a list of what we have to do for the day, and get dressed. Even a morning religious ritual, such as saying prayers, praying with beads (Catholic, Buddhist, Muslim), reading a devotional, or doing meditation can become part of the routine.

When was the last time you asked yourself, Who am I, *really*? More importantly, what makes us ask that question, if we ask it at all?

Let me begin addressing the question of who we are by looking at what is visible to others, our exteriors, before looking at the inner world.

What kind of car do you drive? What kind of car would you drive if you could afford it? Those in advertising would like us to buy the car that says who we are. For the most part, we do. If I ask myself who drives big, four-door, eight-cylinder town cars—the ones with the velvet tops—the answer is, my parents and their generation. When that generation is gone, they will have to stop making those cars. Who buys a Hummer? This is an oft-thought question of mine. What is it that people who buy Hummers want us to know about them? They do want us to think something about them. In the 60s (and even now), who drove Volkswagen vans and Beetles?

Are you what you drive? Does your vehicle, or lack of one, say something about who you are, what you believe, how you live? Even if you say it does not matter what you drive, and you drive a plain, anonymous-looking car, does that say something about you? Perhaps you don't own or don't want to own a car. What does that say about you? It does say something, you know.

Where do you live? What neighborhood? What kind of house, condo, apartment? Does it matter? One patient told me he had to live in a county that was known for its wealth and celebrity status, even though it was a three-hour commute to and from his job.

What kind of clothes do you wear? Do they tell us what kind of job you have, your ideals in life, your desired status? What kind of man wears Hush Puppies, corduroy pants, a pullover V-neck sweater over a tailored shirt, has longish hair to his collar, and carries a worn leather briefcase and some textbooks? We may be wrong, but most likely he is a professor or a student. An article on www.asylum.com, by Alan Wieder, illustrates this point. The article is about a writer, Alan, who will be undergoing a makeover. Here is what he says about his appearance, an appearance he chooses and interprets for us (in case we wouldn't come to the same conclusion):

"All of my life I've maintained a rather disheveled and unkempt-looking appearance: loose, wrinkled clothes; beat-up sneaks; a messy mop of hair; and, typically, a scraggly beard to match. While I'm not unclean, I have the overall look of an out-of-work, perhaps even indigent, humanities professor. ... I dig my rumpled look."[9] Consciously or unconsciously, we choose our outer appearance, our image, and how we want to be perceived. How we look and appear to others is important in defining who we are—or want to be.

When I drive by the hospital and see a plain-dressed man on the street with a stethoscope around his neck, what is it he wants me to know about him? In a medical setting, what is the difference between a short white jacket and a three-quarter-length white jacket? From a friend I learned that the longer the jacket, the higher the status. There is even a white jacket ceremony in the first year, second semester for medical students. Students receive their jackets in a ritual that can be likened to an initiation into the medical field, signifying all the duties and privileges that will go with their jackets. Wearing a short white jacket in a hospital or clinic means something.

What do people tell us by what they wear and how they look, where they live, or what they drive?

It may sound superficial, and maybe it is, but most people, most of the time, identify themselves with the completion of what is expected of them in their society. People adapt to the outer demands of life, to the environment, to the script offered by society, and to getting established in life. In our culture, this means acquiring an education, getting a good-paying job, or becoming a professional, finding a partner, and establishing a home. By the time we are in midlife, many of us have acquired much if not all of the script.

THE DESERT: VULNERABILITY
AND AUTHENTICITY

Being authentic *isn't* easy. In the world of the living, we have a lot to lose. What happens to our identity when our outer world slowly gets stripped away? This is the question of our patients, but also the question of any person who loses their outer image upon which their identity has been built. There is a cost. In the world of the living, each of us has to weigh the price and decide. In the world of the dying, it just happens.

We want to be loved and we want to belong. We want to be accepted. So, we live the script. When at age forty-five, I wanted to live and work in Israel for several years, I encountered great resistance. This resistance came in the voice of my father, who said to me, "You do something like this when you are eighteen or sixty-five, but not when you are in the middle of your career." The script was clear. "Do you realize what it will mean in terms of lost pension and Social Security benefits?" Working with the dying had taught me to pursue my dreams now—instead of later (when it could be too late because of health, finances, or even death). Even in this seemingly small, even insignificant diversion from the normal, I was discouraged. When my father realized that my desire to work in Israel was part of my vocational call, he helped make it possible for me to go, by paying some bills. I could not leave owing any money at all, as I would not be getting paid for my work. How hard it is to be oneself.

We tend to hold on to whatever it is that guarantees us love, acceptance, and safety. This is such a recognized issue that in most pastoral care departments of hospitals and hospices, spiritual assessment forms inevitably list abandonment and isolation as indicators of "spiritual distress." Yet the desire or need for attachment and love, the opposites of abandonment and isolation, should not automatically indicate health. In fact, it may indicate that we are further from our true selves than if we are feeling abandoned and isolated. Buddhism teaches that to hold on to love does not mean we have love. Holding on or being attached simply betrays our opposite need of not wanting to be separated. In the world of the living, the tendency is too often to hold on. In the world of the dying, there is the push to let go. The first world needs to learn from the second world how to let go and how to live.

The suffering that dying people experience is often caused by the loss of the kind of life they had in the world of the living. They are simply unable to hold on any longer. At first, this detaching causes great suffering. For the first time, the old comforts fail to comfort. Those comforts belong to another time and another place. They belong to the world of the living. The dying *no longer have anything left to lose.* They have already lost their future; and in a matter of months, weeks, or days, *they* will *leave* everything behind, even their own bodies. They will leave even those rare but real places, people, and things that they have sacrificed their true selves to hold on to until now. The deception of security crumbles in the shadow of death. For a time, they are alone in a way that we cannot imagine. For many this is the beginning of what theologians call the desert experience. The desert is a place where there is nothing between our self and God. It is a place of transition. It is a place of transformation.

INDIVIDUATION: THE DESERT TREK

A motif or symbol of the archetypal journey of individuation is the desert. It is the most common experience of our patients. Why? Have you ever wondered why after the Exodus it took forty years for the Israelites to reach the promised land? Have you ever wondered why Jesus, following his baptism, was thrust by the Spirit into the desert for forty days (in other words, it wasn't his idea)?

The desert is a place where the question of one's identity emerges. It is the place where the Israelites discovered who they were and where Jesus was tempted to lose sight of who he was.

What did the Israelites take with them, as slaves breaking free and running? What did Jesus have with him? Neither had the comforts of life. The Israelites didn't even have tents, but only some rudimentary and fragile dwelling place that they put together at night and disassembled and carried with them during the day. Today this temporary housing is commemorated by the festival of Sukkot (meaning "booths"), a daily reminder of their insecurity in things, but total security in God. Rabbi Irving Greenberg states, "Sukkot marks the hasty lunches and the endless wandering in the desert. Sukkot expresses the deeper Exodus—the reflective, gritty days of marching ... pitching tents (booths) and taking them down over the course of 14,600 days. Sukkot honors the 43,000 meals prepared on the desert trek, the clean-ups, the washing of utensils. ... Sukkot celebrates a seemingly endless forty-year journey."[10]

Sukkot celebrates a way of learning to live the *no mores*. Sometimes the identities we create seduce us into thinking we are protected, secure,

powerful, and invulnerable. Therefore, the sukkah, by halachic requirement, is to be built upon
no more: no more protection, no more security, no
more illusion of being powerful and invulnerable.
To say it in an awkward way, but one that makes
the point, the sukkah is no more solid walls, no
more shutting out of life, no more acquiring treasures and power and status symbols in the hope
of excluding death and disaster and even the unexpected. Greenberg says that in the sukkah "one
should accept vulnerability and live more deeply,
rather than build thick walls that are intended to
protect from hurt but end up cutting us off from
life. The sukkah does not deny the value of a
solid home or of human effort. ... But the sukkah teaches that builders of homes should be able

to give them up and move out if necessary."[11] Be rooted. Be connected. But be able to move on.

In an interview on the *Oprah Winfrey Show*, Andrew Young, John Edwards's assistant, said that the reason he colluded with Edwards to hide his affair, even claiming Edwards's child with his mistress as his own, was that he was "seduced by the politics, the money, the whole thing." His admission to being seduced by Edwards's power, fame, money, and possible next residency at the White House in 2008, reminded me of Albert Speer, Hitler's architect, whose blind ambition led him to ignore the effect of Hitler's policies on the German public around him, as well as on the Jews. He claimed to be apolitical, caring only about his own career, name, and fortune as an architect. Losing these externals leaves the inner person, however undeveloped, exposed.

Ambition, playing the script that our families or culture has prepared for us in life, and many other conscious or unconscious reasons can cause us not to be our true selves. It seems, too, that age and events can cause us to look for our true selves in our lifetime. A number of individuals have approached me following lectures asking if there is some other way of becoming authentic other than hitting a brick wall that signifies the end of life. Indeed, something in us has the capacity to desire such a quest, although that capacity seems to lie latent until a spark ignites its engine. We can see the great surge of interest in spirituality today: people reading books on Eastern religions—notably Buddhism—doing yoga, going on retreats, even staying for short periods of time in monasteries. While people are caught up in the daily roles they play, they try, at least, to discover a deeper view of themselves, a view from within.

One does not have to be dying to ask the question, Who am I? But most people who are dying ask it, for it is they who live most nakedly, most exposed, no longer able to hide from others or themselves their inner life. Ready or not, wanting it or not, the *no mores* of life have left them exposed, and in that exposure, left some of them confused, disoriented, hurting, and wondering. Like the Israelites, they would gladly go back to whatever kind of life they had before, just to get rid of the pain exposure triggers. In the world of the dying, we call this spiritual pain.

Put yourself in their situation for a moment. This is so important if we are going to understand what the dying are experiencing spiritually. Imagine having your world slowly stripped away. Imagine the *no mores* of *no future* and the slow progression of disease. Imagine losing your job, position, influence, power, personal body image. All the things you have acquired throughout your life are slowly and systematically stripped away. This is an important image, one we can only partially understand in the world of the living.

———◄○►———

MOVIES AND MUSEUMS

If you have seen Holocaust movies, such as *Schindler's List* or *The Pianist*, you have witnessed the slow but systematic stripping away of identity. If you have been to the Holocaust Museum in Washington, D.C., you have seen displays that demonstrate the week by week, month by month, year by year stripping away of Jewish rights with the Nuremberg laws.

We know the most familiar ones—the taking away of the right to work, own a home, be a citizen, sit in a park, eat at restaurants. There were hundreds of laws enacted to strip Jews of their right to live, their right to be. Finally, they were removed from their homes and placed in ghettos. They could take little with them. The crowding and conditions were deplorable. Food was scarce. Disease and starvation were rampant, killing many.

For those who survived the ghettos, the final journey was a train ride to a concentration camp or death camp. Here, if lucky enough to have a real shower, inmates were stripped of all clothing, every hair on their bodies was shaved (they looked like many of our patients do now), and their names were taken away. A tattooed number on their forearms was their only identification.

This is the desert experience. It does not always have a positive outcome. Many Israelites died, never making it to the Promised

Land. Many camp inmates died by becoming what Viktor Frankl describes as Muselmänner—people who stopped living and walked around as zombies. They had given up, walked into electric barbed wire, or simply stopped living. They were stripped of all that was important to them in their lives, of all that gave their lives meaning. And it destroyed them. The desert is a place of decision. It can be the decision to transcend devastating circumstances. It is the story of Saint John of the Cross's *Dark Night of the Soul*. It is the story of Dietrich Bonhoeffer, Viktor Frankl, and every patient.

———◆———

STRIPPED OF EVERYTHING

The world of the living does not know what it is like to be stripped of everything. We can experience one loss, or even several losses at a time. If we do the work of grief, we feel the impact, face the disorganization in our lives that loss brings, and accommodate the loss and move forward. In these losses, other parts of our world are still held intact. The dying, however, experience one loss after another, in rapid succession. Because the losses do not stop coming—because the whole will fall apart piece by piece, preempting any possibility of accommodation and movement forward—the dying are thrown into existential suffering. They are like an onion being peeled away, one layer at a time. Each layer's absence brings its own surprise, in that it is expendable and not essential. Each loss prompts unanticipated reflection and questions: "But if this isn't who I am, if I no longer am doing this or being this, then who am I? What is my essence?"

I can only imagine that at first this is very depressing. But I am not in the world of the dying. Today, I am a pastor with a small church. The people in my congregation respect and love me. From them, I receive nurture and a sense of well-being. I have worked hard over the years to acquire a number of academic and professional degrees. These degrees have given me a sense of identity. With them I carry different levels of authority and expertise. Each sermon that I preach, for example, is a hard-won and novel creative endeavor. I pride myself on making connections, being an original thinker, and having a you-could-hear-a-pin-drop delivery style that engages my listeners and prompts them to reflective thinking and conversation. In this routinely creative process, I receive inner fulfillment. This meaningful process repeats itself in the oral presentations I give as part of the speaking endeavors of my Brick Wall 2 work. If this routine ended, if I were no longer able to speak publicly, or think creatively, or physically get to my speaking engagements, or if I lacked the energy or mental capacity to do any of it, I would feel a partial loss of identity. I receive a lot of affirmation as well as social contact—from my church work and speaking engagements. I am invited to speak at new places where I meet new people as well as keep up with present contacts and friends. The conversations and questions spurred by my presentations also create new excitement, new thoughts, and potential new projects for me. But this is only one layer of my life. The list is lengthy for me, and for each of us, as to what defines us. When the layers of what I have needed to define me are all peeled away, what is left? Who am I?

THE GREAT STRIPPING AWAY

The world of the dying has enlightened me and helped me to make a significant connection between the phenomenon of stripping away of the material world (what I will call the great stripping away) and the emergence of the deeper authentic spiritual self. It is common knowledge among those who work with the dying that *as the dying are slowly removed from the world of the living and decline physically, they bloom spiritually.* Yet, a connection has not been made, as far as I know, between physical and material detachment from the world and the emergence of a deeper spiritual self outside of the world of the dying, except perhaps in the world of the religious ascetic. The dying helped me to see this connection in other lives, in the religious ascetic, and the importance of this phenomenon for our lives too.

"Who am I?" seems to be a question of youth. Erik Erikson developed a now well-known theory of identity development, which posits identity crisis as a normal developmental stage during adolescence, a period between childhood and adulthood. Yet, questions about one's identity can arise at other crossroads or turning points in one's life.

This was true for my own religious identity during the contentious civil rights movement of my teens, in which churches and church members had to decide which side of the aisle they were sitting on—the side that supported the status quo, or the side that protested against the status quo for theological reasons and thus supported racial inclusivity. For me, there were new voices in politics and religion, notably that of Martin Luther King, Jr.

What I have learned from the world of the dying is that when you hit the brick wall and know you are about to die, questions and thoughts arise that could not have been anticipated.

VIKTOR FRANKL

Viktor Frankl experienced what most Jews did in the Holocaust—the progressive and increasingly severe stripping away of the Jewish world and identity.

Frankl's personal journey exhibits this great
stripping away that opens up a deep spiritual place.
We can know what Frankl had and achieved in his
life by what was taken away from him. Born in
1905, he was stripped of his medical credentials
when the Nazis annexed Austria in 1938. He was
stripped of his office and of the special custom-
built desk housed in his sister's apartment when
the Nazis gave her apartment to a German family. He was stripped of a wider medical practice
when the Nazis restricted his patients to Jews
only, even though he was no longer considered
a member of the medical profession. Obtaining
a marriage license immediately before they were
no longer available to Jews, Frankl married Tilly
Grosser in early 1942. Rather than let the Nazis

have their wedding rings when in the same year as their marriage they were deported to a concentration camp, they willingly stripped themselves of them by throwing them out. Frankl's mother, father, and brother were also deported. Tilly was pregnant. They were stripped of their luggage upon arrival at the camp. Frankl was stripped of the manuscript that he had hidden in the lining of his jacket when all Jews were forced to strip and shower. Once showered, Frankl, like all Jews, was shaved of all hair on his body and given rags to wear; numbers were tattooed on his arm, stripping him of his name.

I had never connected the loss of civil and human rights, home, country, belongings, and the incarceration and eventual murder of Jews as a great stripping away that opens a spiritual well within. In his book *Man's Search for Meaning*, Frankl talks about how this great stripping away caused many an inmate to kill himself or drown in despair; but he also talks about the generosity, the help one inmate gave to another, the encouragement and hope that for him are evidence of the one thing left that cannot be stripped away: "Everything can be taken from a man but one thing: the last of the human freedoms—to choose one's attitude in any given set of circumstances, to choose one's own way."

Frankl opened my eyes to those many of our patients who are dying before us, emaciated, bald (but due to treatment, not cruelty), and progressively stripped of almost everything dear to them, even their own body images, yet who find the courage and energy to take hold of this great emptying to see their lives with such clarity that they can and do respond to life and loved ones with honesty and authenticity. *Without* so much of what defined them, it is no mistake that the dying become more blunt, genuine, and authentic. What is left after the great stripping away is just that: no frills, no escapes, no denial, no excuses, no certainty, just the birth of *being* without acquisition, and *being* without *doing*.

DIETRICH BONHOEFFER

Viktor Frankl was a Jew whose fate as a Jew— the great stripping away—was decided by the

Nazis, not by him. Dietrich Bonhoeffer was not a Jew. He was a young German Lutheran pastor and theologian during the Third Reich. He was a man of breeding and privilege. Yet he refused to hide behind these for his own advantage. Instead, he gave them up. Bonhoeffer in Germany, Frankl in Austria. Both men would lose everything and in the process discover that authentic identity can result in spite of what others take from us and in our refusal to be what others expect of us.

Bonhoeffer was born in 1906 into an educated, middle-class German family of esteemed and successful forefbears and contemporaries. Thirteen-year-old Dietrich endured the shock and disapproval of his family when he told them he wanted to study theology, a subject they thought was a path of least resistance and quite boring.

By the time he was twenty-one, Bonhoeffer had already completed his theological studies, his first of two doctoral dissertations, and his pastoral exams. He ventured to Barcelona, where he would fulfill his pastoral internship. He returned in 1929 to a Germany growing in nationalistic fervor with the accession of the Nazis in the elections. He finished his second doctoral dissertation and accepted a fellowship to teach at Union Theological Seminary in New York City in 1930. He was often sought out to give lectures on what was happening in Germany and on the prospects of another war.

He returned to Berlin in 1931. There he taught theology at the university, to students who leaned toward linking Nazism to God's will, and to a German church that was growing in its allegiance to Nazism and *völkisch* ideology (an ideology that emphasized one uniquely German folk spirit).

As the German Christians became more *völkisch*, Bonhoeffer turned to ecumenism and joined with church groups such as the Confessing Church, which opposed the Nazification of the church. For instance, the Confessing Church opposed a resolution at the general synod to adopt the Aryan paragraph (ousting from the synod "non-Aryans" [Jews] who had converted to Christianity and were pastors). This resolution followed Hitler's decree that non-Aryans be removed from all civil service positions in Germany in 1933. It was this decree that cost Viktor Frankl his medical license. And now it would cost Bonhoeffer his opportunity to be a pastor in Germany.

"I have always wanted to be a pastor," Bonhoeffer told Karl Barth in 1933. But he let that dream vanish to stand in solidarity with non-Aryan pastors who were excluded from serving as parish pastors. Bonhoeffer's loss was palpable. "I found myself in radical opposition to my friends ... increasingly isolated with my views of the matter. ... It was time to go into the wilderness for a spell"—as if he wasn't already thrown there. He left Germany to serve German emigrants in

London and spoke out and encouraged protests against the church at home. A 1934 "muzzling decree" by his church made it illegal for him to speak out or write about the church struggle. But that didn't stop him. He asked fellow clergy to separate themselves from the German Christians, without fear of the "possible disagreeable consequences."[12] Most went along though, so as not to lose salary and pension and not to appear disloyal to the state.

In 1935, Bonhoeffer was asked to direct the illegal Confessing Church's seminary at Finkenwalde. It was here that Bonhoeffer wrote the book we studied as teens in our youth group, *The Cost of Discipleship*, and here that he would take these hundred or so seminarians deeper into the wilderness. Bonhoeffer would impose a new kind of monastic existence—more *no mores*—on a world of fewer outside distractions: study, personal confession, group meditation, worship, prayer, and communal living, and the occasional swimming, ping pong, music, and lively discussions. When another church synod proposal sought to endorse the 1935 Nuremberg law that would take away the citizenship of non-Aryans, the Finkenwalde seminarians protested against it. This seminary would not last for long though. In 1937, the Nazis closed it down as illegal; most of the seminarians were conscripted; and most died in the war. Not long after, in 1939, after the church's silence following Kristallnacht of November 9–10, 1938, Bonhoeffer left again, this time for New York City.

Realizing this was a mistake and that he needed to be in solidarity with his brethren in Germany during the war if he hoped to help rebuild Germany and the church after the war, he returned after one month.

In 1939 he joined the military intelligence (the Abwehr), which was exposed only later as the center of anti-Hitler resistance. He was acting as a double agent while avoiding active military service. His actions were being monitored by the Nazis, however, and he lost his right to speak in public in 1941 for "activity subverting the people," and write or publish in 1942 "due to lack of the requisite political reliability."[13] He was banned from Berlin except to visit his parents there in their home there.

His work in the Abwehr cost him friends who believed he had defected to the Nazis. He was without a home, unsettled, and lonely. He traveled undercover, wrote his book *Ethics*, and was involved in Operation 7 (getting fourteen Jews to safety in Switzerland) through his work with the Abwehr.

Thus far, Bonhoeffer's great stripping away had been brought on by his own decisions and actions. He experienced the cost of the discipleship he wrote about. He had not yet asked, *Who am I?* because he had come to know who he was as a Christian and a German. He had chosen Christ over the church, a church which had submitted itself to Nazi values.

Now, however, his freedom was taken from him. He was placed in a seven-by-ten-foot cell in

Berlin's Tegel Military Detention Center, with only a wooden bed, chair, stool, and bucket. He briefly thought of killing himself. He missed his friends, colleagues, fiancée, and work. The stripping away was almost impossible for him to bear.

The prospect of getting married gave him something to hope for, as did the hope that his involvement in the Abwehr's attempts to assassinate Hitler would succeed. He studied the Bible; meditated; read church history, literature, science, and philosophy; listened to music; exercised; played chess with the guards; ministered to other inmates as their assigned orderly; and wrote letters (getting them out through illegal means) to his fiancée, parents, and best friend and colleague, Eberhard Bethge. He began writing theological manuscripts, a novel, and a play. Over a year later, on July 8, 1944, twelve days before the failed assassination attempt on Hitler's life that would seal his fate, he wrote one of ten poems from Tegel, entitled "Who Am I?"

I first read his poem as a young teen in my church youth group. I wondered why a thirty-eight-year-old pastor and theologian, who was certain in his faith toward God, would write a poem called "Who am I?" We were reading one of Bonhoeffer's books and studying his life. I remembered thinking, *Why doesn't he know who he is at his age?*

Bonhoeffer's poem asks the question of identity: "Am I then really all that which other men tell of? Or am I only what I myself know of myself?"[14] What is it that causes him to ask this question now? It is the *no mores* of sights, sounds, and feelings that he includes when he defines how he sees himself:

> . . . yearning for colours, for flowers, for
>   the voices of birds,
> thirsting for words of kindness, for
>   neighbourliness,
> trembling with anger at despotisms and
>   petty humiliations,
> tossing in expectation of great events,
> powerlessly trembling for friends at an
>   infinite distance . . .[15]

Did this next level of *no mores*, the ones he did not orchestrate himself, open up a spiritual place in him that he had not experienced before, so that he revisited the question of adolescence? His poem carries great pathos and power because he did not try to answer the question he posed.

In April of 1943, the Abwehr was brought down by Heydrich's Reich Security Central Office (RHSA), a rival secret service agency of the Third Reich. Everyone was arrested. The discovery of documents confirmed Bonhoeffer's part in the assassination plot, and Bonhoeffer was moved from Tegel to a five-by-eight-foot cell in the basement of the RHSA, where he lived with only a bed, chair, and bucket for four more months. How Bonhoeffer went to his death perhaps helps us understand the last line of "Who Am I?"

The prison doctor described Bonhoeffer as he was being led to the gallows:

> Through the half-open door in one room of the huts I saw Pastor Bonhoeffer, before taking off his prison garb, kneeling on the floor praying fervently to his God. I was most deeply moved by the way this unusually lovable man prayed, so devout and so certain that God heard his prayer. At the place of execution, he again said a short prayer and then climbed the steps to the gallows, brave and composed.

Bonhoeffer's poem ends with the words the prison doctor seemed to witness: "Thou knowest, O God, I am Thine."

Bonhoeffer and Frankl came to different conclusions about what is left when everything is taken away. What we know from the dying is that those who face death can once again return to the central question of identity. The answer unfolds for each person. Let me tell you the story of the patient who taught me this.

SUSAN

Susan was a thirty-five-year-old woman, married with three children. She had breast cancer that had metastasized to her brain. On one visit I made to her home, Susan expressed anger at herself. She told me that in her marriage she had always done what her husband wanted, moved where he wanted to, vacationed where he wanted. She never argued with him or gave contrary opinions about how to raise the children or about religion or politics. "I was always afraid that if he knew what I really thought, who I really was, he would leave me. Now," she said with a slight smile on her face, "I think I'm going to tell my husband exactly what I think. What's he going to do—leave me?" The smile left her face immediately, and in all seriousness she contemplated, "Actually, I am going to do the unthinkable. I am going to leave my husband." She would be leaving him through death.

Susan's comments were very instructive. In the world of the living, we have much to lose by being ourselves, and sometimes we conclude that the risk is just too great to take. Our need to belong and to be loved is so great, it takes a lot of courage to face the possible loss of this need in order to be ourselves. This is why there are so many secrets and lies within families. How often does a spouse know that his or her partner is having an affair, and the partner knows the other knows it, but no one says anything? How many gay adult children never told their parents that they were gay, although the parents, even independent of one another, suspected or knew, but said nothing? Once something is spoken, it gains power and it has to be dealt with. What is not spoken allows for denial, secrets, and lies, and for us to hold on to that which we so desperately desire, but at great cost.

BEING MYSELF: BELONGING

Murray Bowen, family systems theorist, rightly determined that our deepest needs are to *be ourselves* and to *belong*. He called this *differentiation*. Decades ago, I read an article called "Differentiation of One's Self from One's Family of Origin." The author was "anonymous." Only after Murray

Bowen's parents were both deceased did he put his name to the article. I guess that says it all, doesn't it? He struggled with differentiation himself, with being able to be his true self and also be loved and accepted by his parents.

Differentiation is a developmental task on the journey toward individuation. It causes much suffering, because of its potential to keep us from becoming our true authentic self. This is one of the main reasons we have tribal conflicts throughout the world. The need to belong to a clan, tribe, race, nationality, religious group, often preempts any attempt to be critical of one's own. The late John Sanford, Jungian psychologist and Episcopal priest, said, "This tendency to submerge ourselves in the group is a principal source of our remaining unconscious and may exist with our church, our family, our nation, our business, a branch of the armed services, whatever it is with which we identify and in terms of which we define ourselves."[16]

And, I add, for living in the forgetfulness of being. In *Necessary Losses,* Judith Viorst writes about this tendency as an attempt to extinguish the self:

> Our pursuit of this connection—of the restoration of oneness—may be an act of sickness or of health, may be a fearful retreat from the world or an effort to expand it, and may be deliberate or unaware. Through sex, through

religion, through nature, through art, through drugs, through meditation, even through jogging, we try to blur the boundaries that divide us. We try to escape the imprisonment of separateness. ... For it's hard to become a separate self, to separate both literally and emotionally, to be able to outwardly stand alone and to inwardly feel ourselves to be distinct.

IN THE WORLD OF THE LIVING TOO

Our corporate world and global politics are witnesses to the failure to stand alone and experience separation. Jerry B. Harvey, professor emeritus of management at the George Washington University, powerfully illustrates the dynamics of collusion, or agreement, among management personnel, whose loyalty to the organization can lead to immoral or unethical behavior toward its employees—examples such as unjust firing of employees—not for any wrongdoing but for the "greater good" of the organization. He cites the story of a university in a financial crisis, whose faculty heads were approached by the head of the Committee for Finance and Administration for their support in firing senior professors of another department, which was deemed expendable, as the remedy. His friend, the head of the business department, was approached in a way that used the powerful need of human beings to be attached and belong to entice loyalty. He was courted as one of the inner circle, as one whose department would be safe from being fired because they were valued and made money for the university. He was also told that the firing of the senior professors of the humanities department was for the greater interest of the whole university and, finally, that his loyalty to the decision-making body was expected. His friend chose to defend his colleagues who were about to be fired, on the principle that it was wrong. His principled refusal to sell his fellow professors down the river led the head of the Committee for Finance and Administration to rethink his own proposal and called out the nascent humanity principle "to behave morally," states

Harvey. Harvey concludes that "the dynamics of villainy are associated with our instinctive need for attachment and support from the other whom we trust and the reciprocal fear that our need for attachment will be violated by separation."[17]

PHILADELPHIA

How wonderful to be raised in a home that encourages, nourishes, and supports the individual. In *Philadelphia,* Andrew Beckett (played by Tom Hanks) was supported by his mother and father and sisters and brothers when at a family meeting in his parents' living room he told them the trial might reveal difficult things for them to deal with and he wouldn't go through with it if that's what they wanted. He was suing the law firm that fired him for discrimination, believing that they let him go because he had AIDS and not for any wrongdoing. "Son," said his father, "the way you and Michael have dealt with everything with such courage and integrity, I will always be proud of you." "Go for it," his mother added.

I cried! And I asked myself, "Only in the movies?" What of the parents who would not be supportive of their son in this situation? Are they not most likely to be influenced by the larger clan of society, whose values and principles exclude who their son is? Are they not willing to sell their love for their son, to refuse to accept the embarrassment that he will cause them, in order to have the acceptance of the larger clan? How hard it is to know that much of our allegiance to the groups we belong to is based on the fear of being alone.

THE GENUINE

Those of us in the world of the living are attracted to the authentic in the dying person. Why? What longing does it expose in us? When the BBC interviewed Princess Diana on why she visited people who were dying and why she was attracted to hospice care, she said it was because "in this population you meet people who are real." In being authentic, the dying become what they wish they had been all their life, and find true happiness. In contrast, when they thought life was never ending, and when they thought living their truth would cost them, then they were living unconsciously, holding on to and protecting their needs instead of cultivating their truth. Many of us live parts of our lives, or our whole lives, as lies. We want to be preferred, promoted, approved of, and loved.

We should not be casual about how difficult it is to take the road less traveled. Scott Peck's bestseller by the same name touches that part of us that yearns to be an individual who steps to the beat of a different drum, who yearns to be the nonconformist, who wants to take the harder yet more fulfilling way. But real life, in its many personal and professional paths, takes our souls and weaves and intertwines life's many personal and professional roles and loyalties in such a way that cutting even one of its fragile threads can undo the security we have built up all our lives. Some people read the book because they can't live it. When we are really threatened with loss of love and loss of job and loss of security, however we define it, it is hard to stand alone. It is like being naked, being vulnerable. When *Time* magazine claims its person of the year is three women who were whistle-blowers in their corporations, they are by doing so saying how rare it is, how they stick out, how they are to be admired and emulated. But oh, how hard it is to be authentic!

CHAPTER 6

ANGELS, BUSES, AND THRESHOLDS

Do you see the angel sitting over there in the corner?" asked a patient of mine.

"No," I said. "The angel isn't there for me. It is there for you."

"It's been there all day long," she continued calmly, "just watching over me."

It's our clue that they are about to die. In the very last days or hours of life, those who are dying have experiences that are outside the realm of our consciousness. In their 1992 book *Final Gifts*,

Maggie Callanan and Patricia Kelley, two hospice nurses, use the term *nearing death awareness* (NDA) to describe experiences that belong to those who are *actively dying* (when the body begins to shut down at the very end of the dying process).[18]

Our patients or loved ones may report a variety of phenomena—visits by angels, discussions with dead loved ones, taking trips or using symbols of travel—and express exactly when they are going to die.

ANGELS IN WORLD RELIGIONS

Religious Jews do not blink twice when the Hebrew Scriptures tell of the angel Gabriel interpreting meaning for Daniel or giving courage to Enoch on his journey. Christians don't blink twice at Christmas, when this same angel Gabriel comes to Mary to tell her not to be afraid, that the child she is bearing is from the Holy Spirit. It does not even come to our minds to dismiss the reality of this angel Gabriel, who then visits Joseph to tell him not to be afraid to marry Mary, or who visits Elizabeth, Mary's cousin, to tell her not to be afraid.

Gabriel's primary job is to give courage to individuals who are afraid. In Islam there is also an angel who revealed the Qur'an to the prophet Muhammad. Gabriel, as well as other angels, transcends time, faiths, and cultures to do their work.

WAITING FOR THE BUS

Julie was sixty-five. Her mother, who was dying, was in her late eighties. Julie had recently moved her mother into her own home to be with her while she was on hospice care. When I arrived to visit, Julie was visibly shaken. "Something happened last night that frightened me." We sat as Julie told her story.

"It was 2:00 AM. I was sound asleep. Mom was in her room, which, as you know, is next to mine. I heard a loud thump. I hurried into Mom's room, thinking she had fallen out of bed. But she was sitting on the chest at the foot of the bed. I asked, 'What are you doing, Mom?' She answered so strangely. 'I'm waiting for the bus.'"

"What happened next?" I asked.

"Well, I got kind of angry at her. I told her she was ridiculous. That it was 2:00 in the morning. That she was in my house. That she was safe, and that she wasn't going anywhere. I told her to go back to bed." Julie stared hard at me. "What was that about?"

"You and your mother haven't talked about her dying, have you?" I inquired.

"No," she answered, "we haven't ever spoken about it. I'm afraid that she doesn't know she is dying. I try to keep things as normal as possible. She thinks she is here just until she is strong enough to go home."

"You really think she doesn't know?" I asked.

Julie didn't respond.

"Did you notice the words that you used last night when speaking to your mother? You said, 'Mom, don't be ridiculous. You aren't going anywhere. You're safe here.'" I paused for a moment and gently said, "Are you sure you weren't speaking to yourself, Julie, and not to your mom?"

Julie broke down and sobbed. "You think she knows?"

"I think your mom was trying to tell you that she knows, by telling you that she is leaving, and that she is ready to go. That's what 'waiting for the bus' means. But she's afraid for you, Julie. You haven't spoken to her about it. She probably wonders what will happen to you once she dies. So she tried in a symbolic way, a softer way, to see how you would respond. Your response let her know you aren't ready to let her go."

Julie continued to cry. I got up to sit nearer to her. She took my hand. "Oh, Kathleen," she said, "I only wanted to make her feel better by saying what I did. I didn't think she knew she was dying. Or that she might want to talk about it. I love her so much. It's too late now. My poor mother, she must feel so alone."

"It isn't too late, Julie. You can revisit last night with her. Just bring it up again. You can tell her you've been thinking about what happened last night and that you'd like to sit and wait for the bus with her. Does that sound like something you can do?"

Julie did just that. The floodgates opened, as her mother embraced her, crying. They both were able to say things that needed to be said before Julie's mother died a day later. Julie never did find out where the loud thump came from.

Many people at the end of life die alone and with goodbyes unsaid. Symbolic language is sometimes the way the dying tell us in the world of the living that they know they are dying, that they are about to leave, and that they would love to say last things and say goodbye, if only we would let them.

NOT WITH YOU

Ron had been the chief executive of a large company, and even in illness he had an imposing presence. At sixty-nine, he was dying. His hospital bed was in the living room on the first floor of his house. He was unable to navigate the steps that led to the second floor, where his bedroom was and where he did not want to be stuck and isolated all day long. His wife, Mary, continued to sleep upstairs in their bedroom.

Mary was visibly upset when I arrived at her back door for a scheduled visit with her and Ron. "Let's sit down before we go in to see Ron," she said as she waved me to a seat at the kitchen table.

"What's wrong?" I asked.

"Something happened this morning, and I don't know if I did the right thing," she said. I had known Mary for quite some time by now, and I knew her as someone who was very thoughtful in her words and actions.

"What happened?" I asked.

"Well, when I got up this morning, I came down the stairs and, as I usually do, I went over to Ron to say good morning and to give him a kiss. He jerked away from me and said, 'You're being awfully rude.' He pointed to the sofa and said, 'Can't you see my father sitting over there on the sofa? Can't you say good morning to him?'"

"How did you respond?" I asked.

"I looked over at the sofa," she started, "and of course, I didn't see anyone. His father's been dead for twenty years. So I said, looking at the empty couch, 'Good morning, Dad.' Then

I looked back at Ron and asked, 'Honey, what's your father doing here?'"

My eyes encouraged her to continue.

"He said the most out-of-character thing to me. It was so tender. He said, 'He's come to take me home . . . but I'd rather stay here with you!'"

I assured Mary that she did the right thing. She did not laugh at or dismiss Ron as delusional for saying that his father was present. She did not tell Ron that his father was not there. She did not simply ignore Ron. Instead she affirmed Ron and the presence of Ron's father by looking where she was told he was seated and by greeting him. She affirmed Ron again by asking him if he knew why his father was there.

"What happened next?" I asked.

Mary shrugged her shoulders and said, "He kicked his father out of the house."

Two days later, when I arrived at work, I was told that Ron had died during the night. I immediately called Mary to see how she was and to hear from her what had happened. When Mary heard my voice on the phone, she cried as she said, "His mother came for him."

Who do we go with if we do not want to go with the person who comes for us?

HE'S COME TO TAKE ME HOME

If we are not present at the end, if a relative or friend doesn't tell us, or if no one witnesses it at all, we won't know a loved one came to take our patient to another place, a place outside of our realm. Unlike those who have a near-death experience (NDE), our patients do not leave their bodies and venture into another realm and return a short time later to tell us about lights and tunnels and visions or discussions with deceased loved ones. Our patients die and do not come back (unless they "appear" *after* death to console their loved ones—but this is a bereavement issue and not the subject of this book).

It is quite a different experience for our patients who have NDA. For those in the world of the dying, deceased people—those who have already died—or angels *break into this world* from wherever they dwell to visit the dying. We are sometimes privileged to witness our patients talking to someone we are not able to see, or to hear them tell us about the visitors they've had.

DRUGS AND DISEASE
AND HALLUCINATIONS, OH MY!

Years ago, I was at a weekly interdisciplinary team meeting when a nurse spoke about her patient's death, mentioning that at the end the patient died with a smile on her face when her brother, who had died many years before, appeared and took her home. She said this as a matter of fact, as if it were a common everyday experience that did not need any further explanation, and proceeded to discuss the next patient on the census. Our medical director, someone who was often insightful and helpful in the care of our patients, folded his arms over his chest and began to laugh. As the nurse continued to discuss the next patient, he mumbled snidely, "Drug-induced hallucinations." Quite unexpectedly, the nurse snarled angrily back at him, saying that, indeed, the patient's brother had come for her and that the patient was not on any drugs at the time nor had she had any brain metastases. Other team members chimed in, in defense of the nurse, stating that they too had regular experiences of the dead coming for the dying. "You don't see our patients at the very end," another nurse said in her defense. And indeed, he didn't.

Science has a hard time with phenomena of the dead speaking to the dying, or with angelic appearances (let alone with the idea of angels). Yet, many agree that these paranormal encounters are too numerous to be designated as drug- or disease-induced hallucinations.

DELIRIUM OR NDA

Delirium presents with mental confusion, disorientation for time and place, incoherent speech, deficits in attention, hallucinations, short-term memory loss, and aimless physical activity. Patients hallucinating on morphine are totally lost in their hallucinations and do not have coherent conversations with other persons. When dying patients see and speak to angels or dead relatives, it can be misinterpreted as delirium and then inappropriately medicated.

People who are at the end of life and are speaking to dead relatives or angels often involve their visitors in the conversation, even introducing visitors to their dead relatives or introducing living relatives to deceased relatives they have never met before (one patient introduced her adult daughter to her mother, the daughter's grandmother, who had died before her birth). Visitors may feel the presence of another person not visible to them and even interrupt a conversation the patient is having with a deceased person. This is not possible with delirious patients.

The experience of the dead visiting is likely a universal experience of the dying and not delirium or drug-induced hallucination.

THE THRESHOLD

My studies in Judaism introduced me to a fascinating idea. Judaism has rituals for all threshold moments. A threshold is the point where two structures meet, that imperceptible point between this and that, not quite here and not quite there, what Victor Turner calls "betwixt and between," or "neither here nor there."[19]

We have rituals at thresholds to separate out and highlight the transition between two distinct structures of reality, and to provide a way of safely guiding us from one place or structure to the next. The marriage or civil union ceremony is a ritual that marks the end of singleness and the beginning of union. The mezuzah (Judaism) or cross (Christianity), on the doorpost of a house, separates a private space (my home) from the outside world (the public). Baptism separates the "old Adam" from the "new Adam." Havdalah (literally *distinction*) is a Jewish ritual that takes place at the transition point where the Sabbath ends and ordinary time begins. It is replete with wine, prayers, fragrances, song, and dance. Rituals at thresholds also, importantly, transmit and confer identity.

Thresholds are transitions filled with vulnerability and danger. That is why brides (and sometimes grooms) cry at their weddings. That is why elaborate rituals often mark the transition from being awake to falling asleep (notice: "falling") for children (and some adults). The movement from being awake to being asleep is marked by falling out of consciousness. Sometimes we experience ourselves "slipping away" into a sleep state. I recall Rabbi Neil Gillman, a professor from Jewish Theological Seminary of New York, in a class I took with him on Jewish liturgy at Drew University, pointing to children, in particular, as being afraid of this transition. The bedtime ritual may include any number of things: taking a bath (already a ritual of purification or altered identity, as in the waters of baptism or *mikvah*), brushing teeth, having a story read, being tucked in, kissed, told you are loved, saying a prayer, having a night-light on. Some nighttime prayers illuminate the need for protection during this threshold experience. When I was a child, my bedtime prayer was this familiar rhyme: "Now I lay me down to sleep. / I pray the Lord my soul to keep. / If I should die before I wake, / I pray the Lord my soul to take." Talk about being vulnerable and in danger! If the rituals are interrupted for any reason, they must be repeated and completed. If they are missed entirely, children may cry themselves to sleep and have a very restless night.[20]

The point between death and the next realm is a threshold. This breaking into our world by those who have already left it seems to be one that allows the dying to be accompanied over the threshold to their next destination, to another realm. This other realm, this other place, we know little about, and no spaceship can be launched by us to get there. Even those in this world who get a peek now and then through an NDE are forbidden to completely enter.

HOSPICE AS HERMENEUTIC

My experiences with patients have often helped me to interpret stories in Jewish and Christian scriptural texts that I did not understand. For example, I always disliked having to preach on the text called "The Transfiguration of Our Lord." I had read the commentaries, but it still didn't make sense to me—until I worked in hospice.

In this story (MATT. 17:1–9), Jesus knows he is going to die (16:21)—we can liken him to a hospice patient! He is headed for Jerusalem where he knows this will take place, taking with him his three most loved disciples, Peter, James, and John.

On his way, according to the text, Jesus stops at Mt. Tabor in Israel (known as the Mount of Transfiguration). Here, "his face shone like the sun, and his garments became as white as light." Moses and Elijah appear, and Peter asks Jesus if he should build three booths.

First, let me share a little background that helps in the interpretation of this text. When living in Israel, I visited Mt. Tabor and learned from rabbis that this text most likely took place during the Jewish festival of Sukkot, or the Festival of Booths (Peter talks about building booths). It is the first reminder that Jesus is Jewish. Christian interpretations are not cognizant of this Jewish holiday as innate to this text's meaning. If you have ever seen little hut-like structures attached to synagogues, Jewish homes, or even huge office buildings (the Grace building in Manhattan), this signifies that it is the festival of Sukkot.

As I noted earlier, the sukkah is the fragile dwelling structure that the Israelites constructed each night during the forty years in the desert wilderness on their way to the Promised Land. It signifies the endless journey of trust and hope in God. Man-made thick walls of security are replaced by fragile dwellings where the only protection is from God. Jesus, who knows he is about to die, like all of those dying, is vulnerable. The Hebrew Scriptures give exact instructions as to how a sukkah is to be constructed. It must be fragile and open, and *not able* to withstand unusual winds. The sukkah stands as a testimony to human vulnerability, and ultimately, to the need to trust in God, the divine shelter.

"Shall I build three booths?" asks Peter. Judaism has always attested to what attracts many to Buddhism, the urge to give up our false sources of security, our attachment—holding on—to those material things or a certain status, that we think are solid and permanent structures of security. Jesus also said something about not building up treasures for ourselves on earth where moth and rust destroy, but building up treasures in heaven where moths and rust cannot consume. He also said, wherever our treasure is, there also is our heart.

What causes this vulnerability for the dying? The dying are vulnerable because they leave everything. Yom Kippur, or the Day of Atonement, in Judaism, focuses the individual's attention on death, in the belief that facing this threshold experience will move individuals from routine, from taking life for granted, from stagnation, to being mindful that life is a gift—quite like all we have observed takes place for the dying. Yom Kippur is the time when Jews confront death, as Christians do on Ash Wednesday. What pertains to our text, however, is that Jesus' clothes become as "white as light." Why?

On Yom Kippur, traditional Jews put on a white robe called a *kittel,* similar to the white burial shroud. All things pertaining to life are forbidden—eating, drinking, sexual activity, and washing—for a full twenty-four hours. Why are Jesus' clothes "white as light"? Because he knew he was going to die. His ministry was over. He was now in God's hands, totally without the necessities needed to live in the world of the living. The white signifies vulnerability connected with death, and trust, ultimate trust in God only.

Then, the most remarkable thing of all happens. Moses and Elijah appear. I like to say it this way: Two dead people appear. Oh yes, I haven't forgotten. Elijah ascended into heaven without dying. But you get my point. When this text is read during the Western service, no one blinks an eye at the idea.

This is remarkable enough, but it is not the end. Why do these two particular men appear to Jesus (one, dead eight hundred years at that time)? What is the significance?

Ron helped me out here, as did other patients. Who do we want to come for us but those who confirm our identities, those in the end who answer the question, Who am I? Moses was the one who gave the Torah to the people of Israel on Mount Sinai. Elijah was the great prophet, the one still present at special occasions, as the one that will precede the coming of the Messiah.

As if this isn't enough! I was reading the Gospel of Peter, a Gnostic Gospel, not in the New Testament canon. After the crucifixion of Jesus, the text says, two men were at the empty tomb. It was thought that these two men were Moses and Elijah. At the Transfiguration, Moses and Elijah appear. They will journey with him in his dying. They will take him over the threshold to sit at the right side of the Father. They confer and confirm Jesus' identity. He is a Jew on the same important level as they are. Is he the Messiah? Is he the one sent by Jews to be a light to the Gentiles? Who will confer and confirm your identity? Who will come for you?

I have often been asked by Christians who believe in an afterlife and in the resurrection if they will experience the spiritual issues I have outlined in this book. After all, they claim, death is not the end. We don't really die. I remind them of the second-century heretic Marcion of Sinope, who espoused that Jesus, as a divine being, didn't really die, but only appeared to die on the cross (this heresy is called Docetism, from a Greek word that means "to seem"). I remind these Christians that even Jesus knew he was going to die. He gave end-of-life talks (farewell speeches) to his disciples to prepare them for his death and to give them instructions on how to go on without him. At the cross he gave his beloved disciple John and his mother to each other ("Mother, behold your son. Son, behold your mother"), so that they could take care of each other and be there for each other in their loss and grief. There is no resurrection without real death (no Easter without Good Friday) and no reincarnation without real death. Yes, we really have no future here, we grieve the loss of all that is in this world, we have a life review—closure—and we really die.

Afterlife is an experience of the dying, in that the dead from another realm, unasked for and unsought, enter into this world to gently accompany the dying to their next destination.

The dead and angels appear to persons who are actively dying. These are not near-death experiences, but nearing death awareness, a lesser-known phenomenon widely acknowledged as a phenomenon of the dying.

The dead and angels break into the world of the living. This assumes they come from another realm. The idea of an afterlife is confirmed in these experiences and can be comforting both to patients and their family members, as well as to anyone who has feared death. The dead and angels come for those who have a faith tradition (or faith) and for those who don't.

Our role is to educate families about NDA, to normalize the experience, and to clearly document NDA when it occurs.

EPILOGUE

WHAT WE FIND at the end of life is the emergence of a spirituality that could not have been foreseen by those of us not facing death. The news that *I* am dying causes *me* to hit a brick wall, a wall that means *my* end is *really* in sight, that I will *really* die, and that nothing I can do or medicine can do or God *will* do, can change this fact.

Hitting the brick wall prompts a *spiritual shift* in my life. I used to live as if I always had five more years. I lived planning for the next weekend, the next month, the next years, and even further into my future. I took life for granted. I lived it in the "forgetfulness of being." The *shift* that takes place in me is an existential or spiritual shift. I now think about questions I have avoided thinking about my whole life in a deep way: How did I live? Did I have a destiny, a purpose? How did I treat others? Was I loved? Did I love? Was I selfish, kind, thoughtful, mean, or self-centered? Is there a God? Will I be remembered? Where will I go when I die? What does it mean to die?

I may not talk about these questions with anyone, but I am thinking them. I am quiet, not watching TV, not reading newspapers, not listening to music. I'm not interested in what is going on in your world. It isn't my world anymore. I know. I used to be in your world.

I will not be in the future of this world as I used to be. I've stopped planning. I have to cancel plans I've already made. I look depressed, and maybe I am. But my eyes are shut, because I am thinking, working things out!

I am also very sad. I had a lot of plans and a lot that I still wanted to experience in life. I am grieving for all the people I will never see again, all my loved ones, my friends, my colleagues, and my neighbors. I cannot resolve all this grief. It is too much, and I will die before that is possible anyway. I need to talk to some people, write letters to others, video my goodbyes to still others.

I have a lot to do, a lot to ponder. I want someone to visit me and help me sort things out.

Since I found out I am dying, my mind has been going over my past. The past has collapsed into my present, and I am remembering everything: things I had forgotten, things I've said that hurt people, things I've done that have been good. It's a hard job—remembering everything, but now is the time to summarize my life, evaluate what I think about it, and decide if there are things I still need to do, or if I need help in figuring out what to do with what I've discovered about myself. Indeed, it is a time when I am discovering the patterns of my life, and how my patterns of living have affected the quality of my life and of my relationship to myself, to others, and to God. I've discovered that it is these relationships that are most important in life. It's all I think about now. I need someone to talk to about this.

This is my last chance to *see* myself as I really am, to *discover* who I really am, to *decide* who I really want to be before I die, and how I want to be with others and with God. I have never been so detached from the world as I am right now, which is allowing me to think about all this. I've lost my future and all the plans I made. I've lost everything really, my work and career, my freedom to go where I want and do what I want. I don't drive anymore or travel. I can't even go outside to see my garden. I used to have a position, influence, and lots of friends. Not many friends visit me anymore. I'm stuck in my bed. I'm weak. I don't look like myself. I live without almost everything that gave me identity; and I feel so exposed, naked, vulnerable. I can't hide behind anything anymore. So, now I see clearly. Now, I am honest. Now, I have hope to be more authentic than I was in my daily life, and to be more true to myself and therefore to others. Now I become a new person and a gift to myself and to others. I need to talk about this with someone who will listen.

I am not alone. Someone I love or who knows me deeply, and who has already left this world through death, is accompanying me in the last hours of my life. It isn't strange, really. It has happened throughout history and in every time and culture. I go where all flesh goes. I am in community.

———◄○►———

What I have written above is a snapshot of the spiritual world of the dying. The news that I am dying causes me to hit a brick wall, which triggers a shift to a spiritual consciousness. What follows is the realization that I have no future. I am thrown into grief for all that I will lose: all my relationships, all my things, and even my self. In this state of loss—loss of every distraction and attachment—I enter into an automatic state of life review, which is prompted by an innate hope to discover and be my true self and to reach out to others and even to God with that true self, before I die.

At the end of a college course I taught on the spiritual journey of death and dying, the students asked themselves if they wanted to die suddenly or in their sleep, or know that they were dying. The decision was unanimous. While at the beginning of the course they all wanted to die in their sleep or suddenly, now they wanted to know they were dying so that they could have a second chance at life, whose course, direction, and depth only hitting the brick wall could disclose to each of them individually. Yet they knew, and so can we all, that what the dying discover at the end of life is their gift to us now. We don't have to wait to be dying to change our lives now. We can situate ourselves in such a way in life as to allow the spiritual dimension an opening now. Doing so can certainly give us a fuller, richer, and deeper life during our life and not only at the end of our life. Paul said, "I have one last regret: that I didn't live my whole life like this." His regret does not have to be ours.

The spiritual reality outlined in this book is not intended to be the final word on spiritual issues and end of life. It is but one outline, one framework, one pattern of spiritual unfolding, with accompanying stories and theory. Are there more? Undoubtedly there are, and not only other patterns but other spiritual issues as well. My hope is that this framework will spark further and deeper insights into the spiritual dimension of being human, for the sake of our relationship to our selves, others, and God.

NOTES

1 Claire M. Pace, *Description of Suffering as Perceived by Hospice Patients and the Nursing Interventions That Were Effective in Providing Relief*, Fairfield, Connecticut: Sacred Heart University, 2000, p. 30.

2 Calvary Hospital, in the Bronx, cared for dying patients with cancer for over one hundred years. In contrast, hospice care is a model of care that began in 1974 and cares for all the dying, not only cancer patients, and cares for them in all settings—in the hospital, in skilled nursing facilities, and in patients' homes.

3 Hospice Association of America, "Hospice Facts and Statistics," September 2009.

4 R.N. Butler, "The life-review: An interpretation of reminiscence in the aged." *Psychiatry* 26, 1963, p. 66.

5 E. Kübler-Ross, *Life Lessons: Two Experts on Death and Dying Teach Us about the Mysteries of Life and Living*, with David Kessler, New York: Scribner, 2001.

6 The First Temple, built by King Solomon in 960 BCE, was destroyed in 586 BCE, and the Second Temple, which replaced it, was destroyed in 70 CE. Today, the Western Wall in Jerusalem, sometimes called the Wailing Wall because Jews cried there over the Temple's destruction, is the only remnant of the Second Temple.

7 William G. Braude, translator, *Pesikta Rabbati* (2 vols.), New Haven: Yale University Press, 1968, vol. 2, p. 779.

8 Hindrances of the Householder (II), www.urbandharma .org/udharma3/efphholder/efp10.html.

9 www.asylum.com/2010/02/17/a-day-in-the-life-of-sexy -me-one-writer-undergoes-a-man-make

10 Irving Greenberg, *The Jewish Way: Living the Holidays*, Northvale, New Jersey: Jason Aronson, Inc., 1998, p. 97.

11 Ibid., p. 100.

12 Stephen Haynes and Lori Hale, *Bonhoeffer for Armchair Theologians* (Armchair Series), Louisville, Kentucky: Westminster John Knox Press, 2009, p. 37.

13 Ibid., p. 55.

14 *Letters & Papers from Prison*, ed. Eberhard Bethge, New York: Macmillan Publishing Co., 1972, p. 348.

15 Ibid.

16 John A. Sanford, *The Kingdom Within: A Study of the Inner Meaning of Jesus' Sayings*, Ramsey, New Jersey: Paulist Press, 1970, p. 80.

17 Jerry B. Harvey, *The Abilene Paradox and Other Meditations on Management*, San Franciso: Jossey-Bass Inc., 1995.

18 Maggie Callanan and Patricia Kelley, "Nearing Death Awareness: What I Need for a Peaceful Death," in *Final Gifts: Understanding the Special Awareness, Needs, and Communications of the Dying*, New York: Poseidon Press, 1992, pp. 129–72.

19 Victor Turner, "Betwixt and Between: The Liminal Period in *Rites de Passage*," in *The Forest of Symbols: Aspects of Ndembu Ritual*, New York: Cornell University, 1967, pp. 93–111.

20 I am indebted to Rabbi Gillman for my deeper understanding of the significance of thresholds.

INDEX

Kathleen J. Rusnak is known for her warm, humorous, and engaging speaking style, her profound and dynamic content, her gift in making meaningful and thought provoking insights and connections, and for her candor and wisdom.

Choose from the topics listed here or ask Rev. Rusnak to create a lecture on a topic of your choice that is related to spiritual issues.

- ❦ Loss, Grief, and Faith
- ❦ Recognizing Spiritual Issues in Ordinary Language
- ❦ Before They Forget: Recognizing and Maximizing the Spiritual Possibilities of Alzheimer's (CD available)

- After They Forget: The Thriving Spirit of Alzheimer's
- Appearances: Paranormal Experiences at the End of Life and in Bereavement
- Exploring the Spiritual Paradoxes that Shape Healthy Communities
- Caregiving: How to Cope, Care, and Create a Good Life
- Compassion Fatigue: The Professional Caregiver's Dilemma
- Choosing Hope at the End of Life

For more information, visit

www.thebrickwall2.com

or call 603-359-8078

PLEASE VISIT

www.thebrickwall2.com

to order additional copies of this book
or to order the author's other books and CDs.